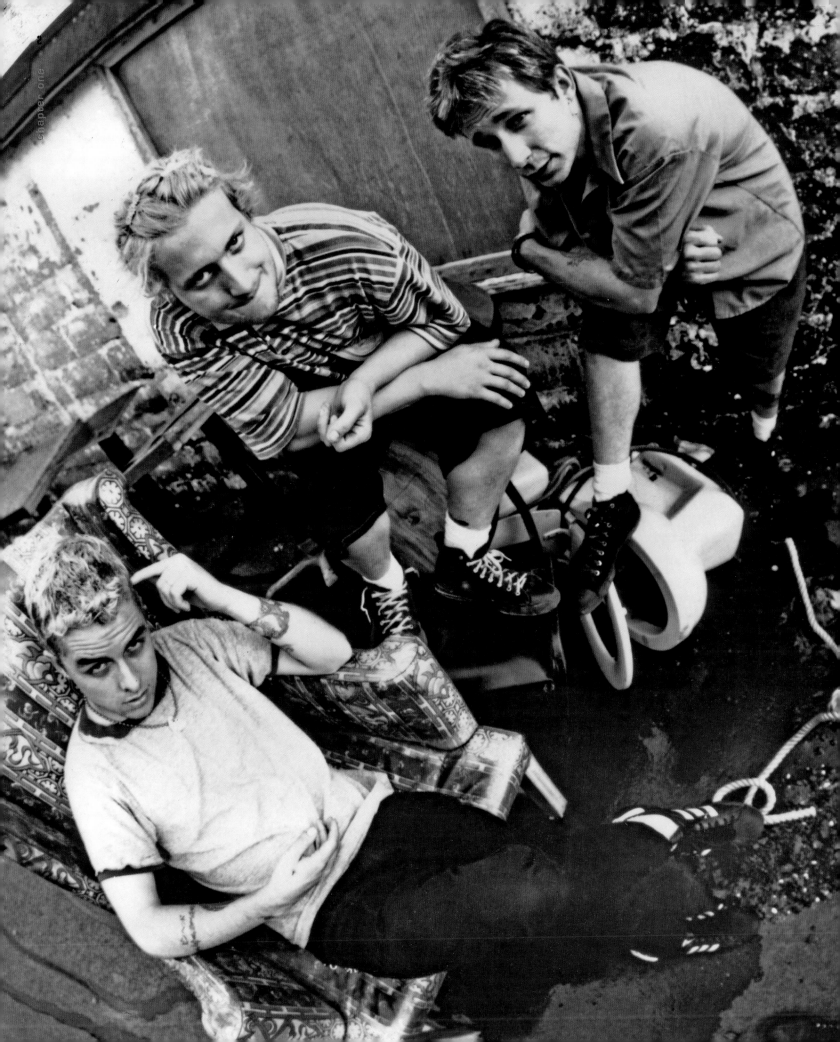

GREEN DAY

the ultimate unauthorized history

Alan di Perna

Voyageur Press

CONTENTS

INTRODUCTION

CADAVERS, COKE-SNIFFING MIDGETS, AND KICKING THE BUMPER OFF A LAND ROVER: WELCOME TO GREEN DAY'S WORLD

In mid-1996—two years after their major label debut album *Dookie* had made them one of the biggest rock acts of the decade and the epicenter of a new phenomenon called pop punk—Green Day were rehearsing in a one-car garage attached to a rundown little ranch house. The house was located in a dicey Oakland, California, neighborhood, right up the street from a crematorium.

Most bands of half Green Day's stature had better rehearsal spaces than this, especially in the '90s. But here were Billie Joe Armstrong, Mike Dirnt, and Tré Cool bashing it out in a cramped, dank space with foam rubber padding on the walls, to which the lads had attached Manowar posters and other scraps of '80s metal band memorabilia. The room was littered with amps, drums, and assorted pieces of music gear, not to mention a large and heavily residue-encrusted bong.

The garage was like something out of *Wayne's World*, some high school kids' boy cave. It's true that Armstrong, Dirnt, and Cool's teen years weren't too far behind them at this point. They were all in their mid-twenties. But, *come on*, these were guys who had toured the world, making a fortune for themselves, not to mention the executive leadership of Warner Bros. Records. They were married men as well. Armstrong even had a kid. *Rehearsing in a crappy garage?* They didn't even own the place; they were just renting it. And they weren't even renting the whole house. Just the garage.

But then, that's the key to Green Day's longevity as a band and their enduring relevance. They've never entirely grown up. While they've matured considerably as musicians and people over the years, they've never let go of that adolescent spark that lies at the heart of all great rock 'n' roll. And Green Day are, indubitably, a great rock 'n' roll band.

Stepping outside the garage to escape the effluvia of stale smoke and sweat was not advisable. For then, one caught a foul whiff of roasting cadavers from the crematorium a short distance down the hill. Not the most pleasant thing for a jobbing journalist who had turned up to interview the band for a feature in *Guitar World* magazine. But at least Billie Joe was amused by my description of the fuel that was feeding the black stench issuing from the large smokestacks just down the hill.

"*Cadaver* . . . I like that word," he pronounced. "Sounds like a big bird or something."

ENTERING MOSHING AREA
IS AT YOUR OWN RISK

Billie Joe and Mike outside their rehearsal space—and uphill from the crematorium. *Guitar World* photo shoot, May 17, 1996. Jay Blakesberg/blakesberg.com

Billie Joe had rolled up in a 1962 Ford Fairlane that was not exactly in mint condition. Cool in a retro sort of way, but not really a rock star ride. His hair was mainly purple during this particular time period, with swatches of magenta and rusty orange brown around the sideburns. Mike Dirnt, for his part, had driven up in a truly ancient and decrepit late-1940s Ford panel van. Also not a rock star conveyance. Fords, apparently, were the order of the day. Tré Cool was not present at this, my first, interview with Green Day. But I would have the curious pleasure of making his acquaintance a few years down the road.

As Armstrong and Dirnt walked me down to a nearby coffeehouse where we were to conduct our interview, they resumed a discussion they'd been having about new cars their wives were planning to buy.

"I told my wife, 'Get anything you want, as long as it isn't a Mercedes or a Volvo,'" said Dirnt, who went on to express heartfelt disdain for that other yuppie status vehicle, the Land Rover. "I could kick the bumper right off one of those," he spat. He seemed on the verge of turning violent. Fortunately, there were no Land Rovers parked in that neighborhood, which provided no opportunity for him to test his hypothesis.

These were guys who seemed determined to hang on to their working-class roots. They appeared genuinely frightened to be perceived as affluent or successful, although they were both. I confess that I found this a little overdone. As a veteran of the first punk wave in the mid-'70s, and a native New Yorker no less, I was a little wary of this latter-day manifestation of punk rock and its somewhat exaggerated, distinctly Northern Californian sense of political correctness. I guess had some growing up of my own to do.

The coffeehouse that Billie Joe and Mike had chosen for the interview proved to be a total disaster. It was pleasant enough, in a funky, student-ish kind of way, but so clattery and noisy that it was impossible to get a decent recording of our interview. I must confess to thinking, *"Come on guys, this is national media, not some fucking fanzine."* Rather than express such a sentiment out loud however, I simply explained the difficulty of being able to transcribe what they had to say, and asked if we could please go somewhere else.

They were polite, but bemused. "OK, but, uh, where?"

"Let's go back to the garage. At least it's quiet in there."

They acquiesced readily, but when we returned to the garage, they discovered they'd been locked out. The owner of the house had locked the door and quit the premises. The members of Green Day didn't even have a key to their own rehearsal room. *"Christ, these guys are real pros,"* I muttered inwardly.

Dirnt finally suggested that we do the interview in his van. How punk rock can you get, right? It was cold and cramped inside, but as we started to talk, all sense of place and time melted away. Mike and Billie Joe's deep love of rock was readily apparent, as was their knowledge of the subject. These guys were no poseurs. While they were keenly aware, and appreciative, of the Bay Area punk bands who were their peers, their perspective was much larger. Some of their more orthodox '90s punk brethren might have been shocked at some of their musical preferences.

"I'm just a sucker for a good song," Billie Joe said. "I like the Beatles a lot. Lately 'Happiness Is a Warm Gun' is my favorite Beatles song. I like Buddy Holly. And I love the early '60s. I love 'Sad About Us' and 'Pictures of Lilly' by the Who. Those are great songs. I think *Beggar's Banquet* is a really classic record. I like 'Stray Cat Blues.' A good song is a good song. I can't even classify them by genres even. Or even bands. Some bands are consistently good. Others have just one good song. 'Black Hole Sun' was a really good song. I was never really a Soundgarden fan, but 'Black Hole Sun' is a good song. I like 'Pretty Vacant' and 'New York' by the Sex Pistols, 'Stay Free' by the Clash, 'A Little Mascara' by the Replacements. . . . Those are really good songs. I'm not particularly into good songwriters, because everyone puts out crap every once in a while. I just like good songs."

We ended up talking in that crummy van for a couple of hours. It was the first of many Green Day interviews I've had the great honor of conducting over the years. Those interviews form the basis of the present book. Unless specified otherwise, all quotes come from that body of work.

As for Tré Cool, I was first introduced to him when Green Day were working on the *Warning* album in L.A. in 2000. I can recall lurching up Cahuenga Boulevard in a rented BMW with Mike Dirnt at the wheel, driving rather recklessly. (Guess he finally overcame his aversion to German luxury cars. Or was he deliberately trying to trash this one?) By this point, Tré had had a little something to smoke and was feeling mellow in the back seat. To distract myself from thoughts of what seemed an inevitable car crash, I tried to focus on the conversation taking place between Dirnt and Cool.

"The last time I was in L.A., I had midgets sniffing cocaine in my hotel room," said Dirnt. "You know, it's much more tame now."

"You don't see a lot of smokin' midget guitar players," Cool replied. "You don't see a lot of those three-quarter-size guitars. Now a ukulele . . . sounds like 'You can lay me.' What about a balalaika?"

Er . . . right, man.

These days Green Day no longer rehearse in a ratty garage. They've got their own facility, Studio 880, which combines a recording studio, equipment storage, and office space in a large factorylike building. It's in Oakland, in an even worse neighborhood than the garage. Some things never change. The members of Green Day all live nearby. They've never absconded to Beverly Hills or New York's Upper West Side. They've stuck close to their roots. They've kept it real.

Back in the early '90s, no one would have predicted that Green Day would become one of the all-time classic rock bands. They seemed part of a passing fad. Pop punk goofballs. But they've long since shown their detractors the error of their ways. It's been a pleasure and privilege to observe, from a somewhat close-hand perspective, Green Day's remarkable evolution over the years. The youthful exuberance of their early stuff. The hidden gems of their vastly underrated middle years. The blazing revolutionary glory of their two punk rock operas. In a time when rock music has become sadly diminished—shrunk down to a squeaky digital download—Green Day consistently remind us of just how big and important rock 'n' roll can be.

We're lucky they love rock as much as we do.

The irrepressible Tré, 1996.
Mark Morrison/Retna Ltd.

chapter 1

RODEO REBELS

When punk rock first came into being in the mid-'70s, it was a distinctly urban phenomenon—an inside joke, if you will, between New York and London. Gritty as a grim city street, grainy as a Soho or Times Square peep show, punk was conceived by the Ramones, Sex Pistols, Voidoids, Damned, and so forth from an attitude, a perspective on rock, and a set of cultural references far beyond the ken of the average suburban REO Speedwagon or Supertramp fan. That urban exclusivity was an inherent part of punk's original brief. It did not play well out of town.

But as the '80s zipped along in a Reagan/Thatcher cocaine blur, punk rock began to radiate outward from urban centers and permeate the suburbs. As part of this cultural infestation, punk eventually reached the sleepy streets of Rodeo, California—the San Francisco suburb and oil refinery town where Billie Joe Armstrong was born on February 17, 1972.

"Rodeo is only ten minutes from San Francisco by BART [Bay Area Rapid Transit] train," Armstrong ruminated in 1996, "but it's like a completely different galaxy."

Armstrong was, by all accounts, born cute—and musical. As a young lad, he sported a mane of tousled golden locks and a cherubic face. He would never grow very tall, even upon reaching full manhood, something that would enable him to retain a boyish charm and assist him in becoming one of the great punk rock heartthrobs. The heavy eyeliner, Manic Panic punk hair dye job, and mildly sardonic, put-upon air that Billie Joe would adopt in later life made for an effective contrast with his compact frame and winning looks.

Billie Joe would hit his thirties and full maturity at a time when the good life had become increasingly elusive for all but the ultra-rich of the twenty-first century, leaving everyone else feeling a bit small. In this dark time, Billie Joe would emerge as a revolutionary punk rock hero, the little guy not afraid to fight back, to jump up on the barricades and lob the first grenade. Flanked by two stalwart comrades named Mike and Tré, he would revolutionize rock music as well, forging bold new song forms to fit the changing times. His rousing songs would speak most resonantly to the young, always the most put-upon in times of economic crisis and war. The cute little kid from dowdy, air-polluted Rodeo would one day be a hero and champion for disaffected, disenfranchised youths of both suburbs and city. He would bring punk rock to the masses.

WARNING: PUNK MUSIC MAY CAUSE CREATIVITY ~AND~ INDIVIDUALITY

LOOK FOR LOVE

LOOK FOR LOVE

"Billie Joe"

Recorded by "Billie Joe" on Fiat Records

Lyrics by James J. Fiatarone
Music by Marie-Louise Fiatarone

$1.25

◀ At the tender age of five, Billie Joe cut his first record, *Look for Love*, recorded and released (800 copies) by his Pinole, California, music teacher. It was packaged with sheet music featuring a photo of the cherubic Billie Joe.

▲ Young Mike was a devotee of '80s British metal bands like Iron Maiden, to whom the band gave a nod with this T-shirt in 2004. WycoVintage.com

Like other notable revolutionary rock heroes, Billie Joe came from a family and socioeconomic background that he would later, somewhat proudly, describe as lower middle class. His father, Andy, drove a truck for a living and his mother, Ollie, was a waitress. Billie Joe was born into a large and loving family, the youngest of five siblings growing up in a three-bedroom house in Rodeo.

Andy and Ollie were able to foster the musical talent that became abundantly apparent in their youngest child when he was still just a toddler. He began taking voice and piano lessons very early, and he was soon entertaining at local hospitals and talent shows. His rock star potential began to emerge very early on. At the tender age of five, Billie Joe cut his first record, *Look for Love*, recorded and released (800 copies) by a local music teacher.

Andy was a jazz drummer himself (in fact he and Ollie first met at a gig), so the couple were happy to encourage their son's musical leanings. Billie Joe took up guitar at age seven, fingering his first notes and chords on an inexpensive Hondo copy of a Gibson Les Paul. Musically, the Beatles made a deep impression on him from a very early age, an influence that would manifest itself in the concise, melodic songcraft of Armstrong's work with Green Day. Slightly more incongruent, given the direction that Billie Joe's career would eventually take, was an obsession with Van Halen, who were huge in the late '70s, just as Armstrong was taking his first steps on guitar.

Just as Billie Joe discovered music early in life, he also came face to face with one of life's harshest realities at a tender age. His world was shattered at age ten when his father died of esophageal cancer. The illness came on quite suddenly, leaving little time for anyone to prepare emotionally or otherwise. The death took a heavy toll on the family's finances and, most of all, their hearts. The young, impressionable Billie Joe was perhaps hit hardest. The songs he would write in later years have often been charged with a sense of life's frequent cruelty.

Not long after this loss, Armstrong became friends with Michael Ryan Pritchard, today better known as Mike Dirnt. Roughly two years Armstrong's junior, Mike had, in many ways, experienced a more difficult early life. Born in Oakland on May 4, 1974, to a heroin-addicted mother, Mike was put up for adoption immediately after birth. At six months of age, he was adopted by Sheryl Nasser and Patrick Pritchard, but the couple separated and young Mike ended up living in Rodeo with his adoptive mother. Tall and gangly, he always seemed somehow not quite at home in his body. Throughout his life, he would be prone to accidents and illnesses. As if to compensate, he would develop a deeply entrenched work ethic and strong-willed determination and loyalty.

◄ Billie Joe's older sister introduced him to Midwestern alt-rock heroes like the Replacements and Hüsker Dü. "Thinking back," he later said, "those were probably my most influential bands." Green Day would later cover both.

Much like the young John Lennon and Paul McCartney, Billie Joe and Mike forged a close bond strengthened by a mutual sense of loss of key parental figures and a deep-seated passion for rock music. Young Mike was a devotee of '80s British metal bands, such as Iron Maiden and Judas Priest, and soon initiated Armstrong.

The two spent their afternoons playing guitars together in Armstrong's bedroom. By this point, Billie Joe had moved on to a Fernandez copy of a Fender Stratocaster, the much-loved blue guitar he made famous in Green Day's early years. Mike had picked up some guitar rudiments from a roommate of his adoptive mom, but when the two boys first got together, Armstrong was the better player.

"I learned how to play 'Johnny B. Goode' and 'Crazy Train,'" Billie Joe recalled. "And there was this local band called the Upstarts; they had a song called 'Suspected,' and I learned how to play that song. Then I listened to a lot of early Van Halen and I learned how to play 'Ain't Talkin' 'bout Love,' which was like near genius for the age I was at. And one night me and Mike just sat around and I taught him how to play a couple of songs. Now he's a better guitar player than me."

In 1996, not too long after Green Day had established themselves as undisputed leaders of the pop punk genre, I asked Billie Joe and Mike if they were embarrassed by their early metal leanings.

"I wouldn't say it was embarrassing," Armstrong demurred. "I learned a lot from that stuff. I learned what I didn't want to play."

To which Mike quickly added, "I learned what I *couldn't* play."

The fledgling duo's musical direction began to change after Armstrong's elder sister introduced him to the early alternative rock sound of Midwestern bands, such as the Replacements and Hüsker Dü.

"I was really into Paul Westerberg [of the Replacements] and Bob Mould [of Hüsker Dü]," said Billie Joe. "Thinking back, those were probably my most influential bands. I loved Hüsker Dü. I like their later stuff more than their early stuff. I really liked the way Bob Mould's guitar sounded."

But Billie Joe and Mike's fate was truly sealed when they were about fourteen and acquaintances from another outlying Bay Area town gave them their first taste of punk rock. "Their dad lived in the same town we did," Armstrong recalled. "They used to come around, and they started bringing down records like D.O.A. and the Dead Kennedys. Then there was a girl at school, I remember, in the seventh grade, who would bring records in and say, 'Here, listen to this.' And she had stuff like TSOL. And I think I really started getting into punk with a record that *Maximumrockandroll* put out called *Turn It Around!*. It was a double seven-inch and it had bands like Crimpshrine, Sewer Trout, and stuff like that. That was when it really started hitting me. This was around 1987."

▲ "Discovering bands like Crimpshrine, Sewer Trout, and stuff like that. That was when it really started hitting me," Billie Joe recalled. Sacramento's Sewer Trout released "Sewer Trout for President" b/w "Que Sera" on the One Shot Flop label in 1988. Berkeley's Crimpshrine released their Quit Talkin' Claude EP on Lookout! in 1989.

924 GILMAN ST
MAY
in Berkeley

Fri 18 *Fuck Ups* · **Corrupted Morals**
the Blisters (NJ) · Capitalist Casualties · Missing Children
Sat 19 Screaming Sirens · **FRIGHTWIG**
the Fixtures · Lovedog · Cantankerous
Sun 20 (3 pm matinee) **FUGAZI** · Offspring
BEAT HAPPENING (Wa.) · Monsula · Pez
Fri 25 S☮UP (reunion) · Green Day
Brent's TV · Blatz
Sat 26 MDC · Ultraman
the Big Thing (Phila.) · Cracks in the Sidewalk
JUNE
Fri 1 Skankin' Pickle · Cat's Pajamas
Rudiments · Scout's Honor · LessIsMore
Sat 2 tba · Resist · Elegy
Fri 8 the GRIM · the Dread · FFI
Sat 9 Subvert · Misery
Apocalypse · Asbestos Death
Fri 15 *Gargoyles* · Christ on a Crutch
Harsh (LA)

MOST SHOWS at 8 pm for $5
$2 Annual Membership Card required
aLLaGES No Alcohol
showinfo (415) 525-9926
booking (415) 524-8180 7:30-9 pm

▲ A 924 Gilman Street ad that appeared in the May 1990 issue of *Maximumrockandroll*, the influential Bay Area punk fanzine that played a key role in Mike and Billie Joe's lives. Michelle Haunold collection/ GearheadRecords.com

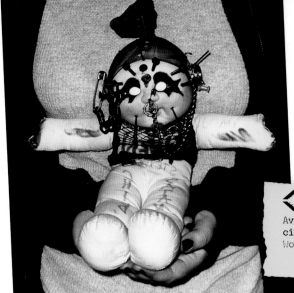

◀ Scene on Berkeley's Telegraph Avenue, a noted hangout for the city's punk rockers. © Larry Wolfley/larrywolfley.com

Maximumrockandroll, the influential Bay Area punk fanzine, and its founder Tim Yohannan, would play key roles in Mike and Billie Joe's lives just a few years down the road. For now, the lads weren't quite ready even for the fanzines. Roundabout the tenth grade, they formed their first band, with Billie Joe on lead guitar and Mike on rhythm guitar, along with school friends Sean Hughes on bass and Raj Punjabi as the first of several drummers.

The fledgling quartet assayed a lot of metal at first, but eventually gravitated more toward their Replacements and Hüsker Dü influences. After a few nomenclatorial false starts, the new band settled on the name Sweet Children, after the title of an early song by Billie Joe. Even at this early stage, he was beginning to explore the songwriting gift that would eventually ignite the pop punk '90s and challenge the corporate monster that would rear its ugly head in the '00s.

Sweet Children underwent a few crucial lineup shifts, but Billie Joe and Mike became increasingly cohesive as the nucleus of the group. Their connection became even closer when Mike's adoptive mom decided to leave Rodeo in search of more affordable lodging and Mike began living at Billie Joe's house. "I moved out of my mom's house when I was about fifteen," Mike recalled, "and moved in with Billie. I rented a room from his mom on the side of his house."

The musical approach that the two friends forged came into sharper focus when Sean Hughes dropped out of Sweet Children and Mike took over bass duties. "When our old bass player went to the dentist one day, I just picked up his bass," Mike recalled. "Me, Billie, and this guy Jimmy we used to play with said, 'Hey, this is much better!'"

"We were trying to teach Sean, who is still one of our best friends today, to play bass," Billie Joe said in 1996. "But he was just a beginner; he tripped over his fingers a lot."

"Billie's brother said to me, 'No matter how many guitar players are in a band, there's always just one bass player,'" Mike added. "And I thought, 'Hmmmm.' It was really natural to switch to bass. I've always liked it as an instrument—bass players like John Entwistle. Not that I'm anything like him! But I've always listened to the bass and heard a counter melody to whatever's going on with the lead vocal. And people like Tommy Stinson [of the Replacements] always looked really cool with a bass in their hands."

Mike would go on to become arguably the best bass player in contemporary punk. As soon as he adopted the instrument, he began practicing assiduously at home and even at school. Which is how he acquired his stage name. Classmates would mimic the sound of his unamplified bass—*dirnt, dirnt . . . dirnt, dirnt*—and Michael Pritchard became Mike Dirnt.

FRI NOV 11

LIBIDO BOYS

SYSTEMS COLLAPSE
TALLY HOE

SWOLLEN BOSS TOAD

924 GILMAN ST BERKELEY

Leave your nacho problems at HOME.

Alternative Music Foundation
Info: 849-0819

Let's Disco...

ALL AGES **$5**
$4 for members

Doors at 8, Sho...

FANG
SKINYARD
COFFIN BREAK
Hester PRyNe

ALL AGES!

No Alcohol

924 GILMAN ST. BERKELEY
#415/ 525-9926 **$5**

THREE SEATTLE BANDS!

SUN. JAN 29th pm

Without Borders: 1989 ANARCHIST Conference & Festival
the TV Generation
...and how to meet the challenge

SF. JULY 19-25

presents
Ⓐ benefit
...All Ages...

924 GILMAN
–Berkeley–
SAT. MAR. 25.
8:30 PM... $5.00

SABØT
Pollution Circus
Christ on Parade
Peter Plate
the HIGH RISK GROUP
Richard Loranger
HANK HYENA

-Music-words-dance-film-

Call for info? 8oh·gosh!

DEFIANT TEENAGER?
Is Your Teenager Irresponsible, Rebellious, Or Out Of Control? Running With The Wrong Crowd? Headed Down A Path With No Future? Help Your Son Or Daughter Before It's Too Late!

WE CAN HELP HER STRAIGHTEN UP. Some kids get into a slump and just can't get out. They become defiant, disruptive and out of control of school.

WE GET RESULTS WHERE OTHER THERAPY HAS FAILED

mentors
GLAMBODIANS
$6
YEASTIE GIRLZ
MISLED

SHOW STARTS **8:00**

minors welcome · no alcohol

FRI, MARCH 2
(415) 525-992

924 GILMAN STREET BERKELEY

Fliers, 1988–1990. Perhaps no place on earth personified the militant idealism of '80s American punk more than 924 Gilman Street, founded by *Maximumrockandroll*'s Tim Yohannon. It was here that punk rock fused with Berkeley's long history of political activism. All Michelle Haunold collection/ GearheadRecords.com

ADOLESCENTS -LA
ATTITUDE: I have ONE !!!
LIFELINE -Formerly S.J.'s FRONTLINE
FORMERLY S.J.'S FRONT-LINE

-AND- BY- NEUROSIS

RIP ROARING RAPAGE PARTY !!!!!
431-1326

$6
THE RIPPINEST ≡1988≡

All Ages Welcome . .
AT- THE BERKELEY SQUARE Dec 29
1333 University Berkeley . . . .

Fliers, 1988 and 1989. Berkeley Square offered
another all-ages venue for punk shows, often
hosting out-of-town bands. Michelle Haunold
collection/GearheadRecords.com

GWAR
OPERATION IVY

OPERATION IVY RECORD RELEASE PARTY 9 P.M.
TUES. APRIL 11

BERKELEY SQUARE
Nightclub and Restaurant
1333 University, Berkeley 849-3374

Things really began picking up for Sweet Children when a local guy named John Kiffmeyer took over as drummer. A few years older than Billie Joe and Mike, Kiffmeyer was a member of the local punk band Isocracy and a well-known figure in the punk scene then coalescing in nearby Berkeley. Kiffmeyer went by the stage name Al Sobrante, a riff on the name of the working-class Northern California suburb where he came from, El Sobrante. Being older and more seasoned than Armstrong and Dirnt, he began acting as Sweet Children's business manager as well. Because he had performed there with Isocracy, Sobrante had an in at an exciting new all-ages punk rock venue named for its street address at 924 Gilman Street in Berkeley.

Mike and Billie Joe had faithfully attended shows at Gilman Street ever since the club opened on New Year's Day of 1987, but they hadn't been able to land Sweet Children a gig there. They'd been judged to be insufficiently punk, apparently. With Kiffmeyer in tow, they were finally deemed worthy, and over the Thanksgiving holiday of 1988, after a small warm-up gig at Rod's Hickory Pit where Billie Joe's mom worked as a waitress, the group soon to be known as Green Day made their Gilman Street debut. In time, both the venue and the band would become legendary, although the latter would far outstrip the former in fame and glory, not to mention finances.

Flier, 1989. With older drummer John Kiffmeyer in tow, Sweet Children began landing gigs Gilman Street. Michelle Haunold collection/GearheadRecords.com

chapter **12**

PUNK IS NOT DEAD

A lot had happened to punk rock in the decade or so that separated the music's first explosion in the '70s and Sweet Children's Gilman Street debut in the late '80s. Initially, punk possessed three distinct strains: the cynical nihilism of the Sex Pistols, the comic book goofiness of the Ramones, and the idealistic political engagement of the Clash. It was the third of these tendencies that became the predominant mode as the punk diaspora spread across America in the 1980s.

Washington, D.C.'s hardcore punk movement of the early '80s had played a key role in pushing the music and culture in a politicized, fiercely idealistic direction. Many hardcore groups adhered to a drug- and alcohol-free "straight-edge" lifestyle. Clear-headedness made one a more effective soldier for the revolution, they reasoned. Some even added celibacy to their definition of punk rock discipline. Much to the bemusement of punk's original and proudly messed-up "Class of '77," punk rock became an almost monastic vocation in '80s America, demanding of its adherents an absolute devotion to the music and lifestyle. For a certain breed of alienated youth seeking an alternative to their parents' anesthetized, complacent suburban lifestyles, militant punk rock orthodoxy was immensely appealing.

August 31, 1990. At 924 Gilman Street, Billie Joe and Mike found a nurturing environment in which to transition from adolescence to adulthood. Murray Bowles

▲ Fronting the band rechristened Green Day, 924 Gilman Street, September 9, 1989. Tim Yohannon, a former campus radical on the East Coast in the '60s, set up Gilman Street on strictly socialist principles. Murray Bowles

7 924 Gilman Street, September 9, 1989. Original Sweet Children/ Green Day drummer John Kiffmeyer— a.k.a. Al Sobrante—was a few years older than Billie Joe and Mike and a well-known figure in the Berkeley punk scene. Murray Bowles

All that discipline gave the scene considerable power. A network of indie record labels, distribution companies, and small venues established itself across America. This allowed bands to bring their music to a substantial and appreciative public without having to sell their souls to a corporate record label, as—it was widely felt—most of the first-generation punk bands had done. While punk's first wave had originated the D.I.Y. (do-it-yourself) ethic, there wasn't much of an independent record distribution network back then. Most of the first-generation punk bands ended up working with major labels, in some cases after an initial indie release or two. But by the '80s, D.I.Y. had become an actual, practical economic and cultural system. No one was making big bucks, but that was precisely the point. If you were in it for the money, you were in it for the wrong reason. The major labels, for the most part, had long since lost interest in punk and moved on to new wave, synth pop, hair metal, and other genres. The late '80s punk scene's modest economy allowed it to survive, albeit under the radar. It became a truly underground phenomenon.

And perhaps no place on earth personified the militant idealism of '80s punk in America more than 924 Gilman Street. It was here that punk rock fused with Berkeley's long history of political activism. *Maximumrockandroll*'s Tim Yohannon had been a campus radical on the East Coast in the '60s, and he set up Gilman Street on strictly socialist principles. Not a bar like CBGB, the 100 Club, or most other historic punk venues, Gilman Street was a co-op. Anyone who attended could become a member; and all members had an equal voice and could vote at regularly scheduled meetings to determine the collective's policy. One of the grounds for expulsion from the co-op, however, was signing a contract with a major record label.

"MAKE THE COLLECTOR NERD SWEAT"
10" COMPILATION RECORD RELEASE PARTY.

PLAID RETINA
THE OFFSPRING
924 GILMAN ST.
AT 8TH IN BERKELEY

ALSO ON THE RECORD:
JAWBREAKER
SAM IAM
the WRONG
CRIMPSHRINE

MR. T EXPERIENCE
LOOKOUTS
COFFEE & DONUTS
CRUMMY MUSICIANS

Very small RECORDS

FRIDAY JAN 5

8PM SHARP!
6 BANDS 6 BUCKS

drawing by sergie. flyer by petey

◄ Flier, 1989. East Bay punk bands from a number of labels were featured on the *Make the Collector Nerd Sweat* 10-inch. Michelle Haunold collection/ GearheadRecords.com

FOR NO APPARENT REASON, IT'S A...
LOOKOUT RECORDS
Corrupted Morals
NOT IN THIS ORDER
...PARTY?
PLAID RETINA
LOOKOUTS
SRROGATE
YEASTIE BRAINS
GIRLZ
EYEBALL
SEWER FUCKIN TROUT
PEOPLE WHO ARE BAD WILL GET SPANKED
KAMALA AND THE KARNIVORES

NEW EYEBALL 7" IN MARCH
NEW SURROGATE BRAINS 7" IN MARCH
KAMALA & the KARNIVORES 7" IN APRIL
LOOKOUTS, PLAID RETINA & CORRUPTED
MORALS WILL HAVE LP's OUT THIS
SUMMER.

SUNDAY FEB
GILMAN 3PM 19TH

► Flier, 1989. Lookout! Records had grown out of Lawrence Livermore's fanzine, also called *Lookout!*. It would become home to a variety of influential bands, including Alkaline Trio, the Donnas, Queers, Screeching Weasel, Groovy Ghoulies, Hi-Fives, and Livermore's own group, the Lookouts. Michelle Haunold collection/GearheadRecords.com

924 Gilman Street,
August 31, 1990.
Murray Bowles

◄ Coming from Berkeley, whose punk scene tended to be less doctrinaire than those in other cities, Mike and Billie Joe did not find punk, metal, and even psychedelia to be mutually exclusive. San Francisco, November 7, 1989. Murray Bowles

Alcohol has never been sold or served at Gilman Street. This policy saved Yohannon the hassle of obtaining a liquor license, which is often an obstacle to opening or maintaining a more conventional rock venue. Of course, bands and patrons could, and did, avail themselves of nearby bars and liquor stores to tank up before entering Gilman. But open drunkenness would result in a firm, if nonviolent, expulsion for performers as well as audience members. Another strict Gilman Street policy was the absolute equality of bands and audience. Musicians enjoyed no special privileges, backstage scene, or cordoned off VIP area. The acts on crowded Gilman Street bills mingled with the audience before and after taking their turn on stage.

This was the environment in which Sweet Children made their official public debut on that late-November evening in 1988, performing the first of what would be many Gilman shows. While they were still pretty green, to coin a phrase, their brief set was a harbinger of things to come. They principally played Billie Joe originals, but also wove in two rock 'n' roll classics (and garage band staples): Chuck Berry's "Johnny B. Goode" and the Who's "My Generation." From the start, Armstrong and Dirnt's frame of reference was broader than the latter-day punk orthodoxy promulgated by fanzines like *Maximumrockandroll*. Sweet Children, nonetheless, made a favorable impression on the Gilman Street crowd. Those who were there remarked on the fledgling group's youth, above-average competence on their instruments and ability to sing vocal harmonies, an accomplishment that eluded most, if not all, other Gilman acts. What no one in that small punk club on a winter's night could have realized at the time was that they'd just witnessed the debut of a band that would eventually go multiplatinum and exert a profound influence over an entire generation.

At Gilman Street, and in the progressive Berkeley/Oakland milieu generally, Billie Joe Armstrong and Mike Dirnt found a nurturing environment in which to transition from adolescence to adulthood. Billie Joe quit school and essentially became a person of no fixed abode, living with friends or in punk rock squats. "My mother wanted me to pay $250 a month in rent when I dropped out of school," he recounted. "I said, 'Nah, I can live somewhere else cheaper than that.' Coming to Oakland was sort of a godsend. I learned more than I'd learned ever before by living in Oakland, sleeping on people's couches and staying in warehouses—stuff like that."

> An early photo of Mike with his beloved Gibson G-3, 924 Gilman Street, August 31, 1990. Murray Bowles

GREEN DAY

1,000 HOURS

Lookout! #17 RECORDS

BILLY: GUITAR, HAT.

A
1,000 hours 2:24
dry ice 3:43

MIKE: BASS, HAIR.

45rpm

JOHN: DRUMS, BOS.

B
only of you 2:44
the one i want 2:59

LOOKOUT
P.O. BOX 11374
BERKELEY CA
94701

In April 1989, Lawrence Livermore brought Armstrong, Dirnt, and Kiffmeyer into the studio to record their debut 7-inch EP, *1,000 Hours*, for Lookout! Michelle Haunold collection/ GearheadRecords.com

A night spent in one particularly dicey punk squat inspired Billie Joe to write one of his best-known songs, "Welcome to Paradise." In a few years, the tune would become a megahit. But at the time, Billie Joe was just happy to make a go of it on his own. It was at Gilman that he met his first serious girlfriend, Erica Paleno. He was sixteen years old. Life was good.

Meanwhile, Dirnt had also begun to drift away from Rodeo while still completing his high school education there. "I moved out of Billie's mom's house," he recalled. "I was going from place to place and then Billie moved to Oakland. We actually met again in Oakland, at a warehouse."

Like Armstrong, Dirnt felt that the exhilaration of living on his own far outweighed the financial challenges. "It's not like living back home, kicking back with Mom," he said. "It's getting out there and trying to score your next meal. Making what fun you can. Working as hard as you can not to work. Which is usually a lot of work."

Building on their Gilman Street popularity, Sweet Children were able to score other gigs locally, mostly at house parties. It was at one of these parties that Lawrence Livermore, who ran the small punk indie label Lookout! Records, discovered them. The label had grown out of Livermore's fanzine, also called *Lookout!*, and had garnered some success with Operation Ivy, a band that would eventually morph into Rancid. Lookout! would become home to a variety of influential bands, including Alkaline Trio, the Donnas, Queers, Screeching Weasel, Groovy Ghoulies, Hi-Fives, and Livermore's own group, the Lookouts. But in 1989, Livermore was still building his roster. He wisely discerned that Sweet Children would make a good addition to the lineup.

In April of that year, Livermore brought Armstrong, Dirnt, and Kiffmeyer into the studio to record their debut 7-inch EP, *1,000 Hours*. On the eve of the disc's release, the trio made a momentous decision. Recognizing the inherent lameness of the name Sweet Children, they decided to rechristen the band Green Day. The new appellation also came from a song by Armstrong and alluded to the band's longtime drug of choice: marijuana.

◀ *Sweet Children*, another 7-inch EP released on Lookout! in the summer of 1990, featured a cover of the Who's "My Generation."

By any name, Green Day's debut recording is remarkably strong for a low-budget first effort by a fledgling band. Most of what would become the key elements of the Green Day sound and style are already in place on *1,000 Hours*, most notably Billie Joe and the band's concise, infectiously tuneful songwriting. The title track's verse melody wouldn't be out of place in a psychedelic garage pop hit from the mid- to late '60s. And the chord progression and vocal harmonies for "The One I Want" are distinctly Beatlesque, although the overall sound and energy level are pure '80s Gilman Street punk rock. The arrangements are tight and well thought-out. Dirnt is rock solid, and each of the four songs features a capable, concise Billie Joe guitar solo. The dexterous solo on "Dry Ice" perhaps even hints a bit at Armstrong's early preoccupation with hair metal.

Billie Joe's lyrics for all four tunes sound a note of forlorn romanticism, pining for a love lost or unattainable. With its moonlit setting, flowers, and silhouettes on a window shade, "1,000 Hours" is steeped in an old-world lyricism that seems oddly incongruent—yet strangely effective—in a punk rock setting. *Let my hands flow through your hair*, Billie Joe sings like some latter-day Lord Byron or Tin Pan Alley songster, *Moving closer, a kiss we'll share*. This strain of emotional vulnerability would prove a key element in Armstrong's persona and songwriting voice.

Two more 7-inch EPs, *Slappy* and *Sweet Children*, followed shortly after, neither as strong as *1,000 Hours*. *Slappy* is marred by a thin sound and some hopelessly sloppy drumming. But one can hear Billie Joe's trademark nasal vocal style, with its unique elongated vowel sounds, coming into increasingly sharper focus. The three EPs ultimately led to the release of Green Day's debut album, *39/Smooth*, recorded over the Christmas 1989 holiday at the Art of Ears studio in Berkeley, where the EPs had also been committed to tape.

LOOKOUT RECORDS   RECORD RELEASE BLOW-OUT:
FOUR BANDS.....FOUR NEW RECORDS!

LOOK FOR LIVE 7" TOO.

NEUROSIS
the
Mr T Experience

LOOK FOR 12" & L.P. ON NEW RED ARCHIVES TOO.

Samiam

DON'T LOOK FOR L.P. ON I.R.S. BUT FLEXI IN THE WORKS.

Green Day

FRI., MARCH 16th.
gilman st.

⊕SERGIE 90

▲ Flier, 1990. Lawrence Livermore had wisely discerned that Sweet Children would make a good addition to the Lookout! roster. A few months later, the trio made the momentous decision to rechristen the band Green Day. Michelle Haunold collection/GearheadRecords.com

A first album poses a challenge to any band. It's a different animal than a single or EP—a major statement. Coming up with ten songs that offer variety, yet somehow hang together in a stylistically coherent whole, requires a band to pull out all their resources as players and songwriters. The three members of Green Day at the time of *39/Smooth* rose to these challenges with varying levels of success.

As a lyricist and tunesmith, Billie Joe takes a few significant strides forward on *39/Smooth*. The forlorn lyrics of the earlier EPs morph into more developed narratives with humor, deft characterization, and a sense of place ("At the Library," "The Judge's Daughter"). Quite a few of the songs deal effectively with adolescent angst and identity issues ("Disappearing Boy," "16," "Road to Acceptance"), a topic that would become one of Armstrong's key songwriting themes. Where earlier punk had riffed on adolescence in a comic book/pop art kind of way, Billie Joe's more straightforward and emotive treatment of teenage insecurities and anxieties would strike a deep chord with audiences of the 1990s and beyond.

Green Day's debut album is also remarkable for containing the tune that gave the band their name, Armstrong's quasi-psychedelic ode to the ganja leaf. And while "Rest," with its slow, ¾ waltz time signature, may not be entirely successful, it does show a precocious willingness to venture beyond up-tempo punk rock formulas. On all tracks, Armstrong is ably supported by Dirnt's tightly honed bass work and growing strengths as a harmony vocalist. Unfortunately, Kiffmeyer's shortcomings become painfully apparent on *39/Smooth*, his unsteady meters and lurchingly awkward drum rolls dragging down the momentum at many junctures.

April 1990

THE ALBUMS

39/Smooth

Green Day's first album is mainly of historical interest today. It is the humble freshman effort of a band destined for greatness. Knowing what Green Day would go on to achieve, it's easy—and kind of fun—to search for diamonds in the rough amid the overall amateur-night mawkishness of 39/Smooth.

As with all Green Day albums to come, the principal attraction here is Billie Joe Armstrong's songwriting. Even at this early stage, his melodic gift is abundantly apparent. "Going to Pasalacqua" and "16" boast particularly catchy tunes. Lyrically, Armstrong mostly dwells on romantic rejection and frustration at this early juncture. But he's already got an eye for ironic twists on this well-worn subject matter. Witness, for example, the dysfunctional romantic triangle in "The Judge's Daughter:" *You're the one I wish I had/Now my girlfriend's getting mad.*

While Billie Joe was well along the way as a songwriter at the time 39/Smooth was recorded, he hadn't quite dialed in his vocal approach. He's clearly straining on "Road to Acceptance," the key being pitched too high for his vocal range. This is a common pitfall for upstart bands, which are often more focused on the guitar riffs than the vocals. Speaking of which, the guitar tone on 39/Smooth is fairly typical of low-budget indie productions. In other words, it's a bit weak and wimpy. Most of the guitar tracks are processed through some kind of flanger or phaser pedal—a frequent security blanket for fledgling guitarists, but one which tends to diminish the instrument's overall frequency range and punch.

While the tone is somewhat anemic, Billie Joe emerges as a pretty wicked little guitarist on 39/Smooth. The harmonic riff in

"At the Library" is clearly the work of a guy who's studied a few Van Halen records. And the solo in "The Judge's Daughter" attains a considerable degree of heat. It's clear, in retrospect, that Billie Joe has been hiding his six-string torch under a bushel for most of Green Day's career. But then hot guitar work *is* completely antithetical to the punk rock aesthetic.

Which is another issue that one may have with 39/Smooth. It's a little bit all over the map stylistically. Just as Armstrong hadn't completely dialed in his vocal sensibility at this point, his songwriting style hasn't come fully into focus either. He's always worn his influences on his sleeve, but his well-documented fascination with the Midwestern alternative pop sounds of Hüsker Dü and the Replacements is perhaps a little too apparent on songs like "Road to Acceptance" and "Don't Leave Me." The latter track's main riff is also a pretty blatant rip on "All Day and All of the Night" by the Kinks—another key Armstrong influence.

It's hard to tell what to make of the slow, ¾ time song "Rest." It seems a failed attempt to sound like some regrettable '70s arena rock act. *What* were Green Day thinking? Structurally, as well, Armstrong tends to favor instrumental breakdown sections in lieu of thoughtfully written musical and lyrical bridges on 39/Smooth, although these breakdown sections often give Mike Dirnt's sterling bass playing a change to shine through.

39/Smooth is also notable for "Green Day," the song that gave the band its name. Marijuana being the subject matter, this is a rare instance of a proto-psychedelic lyric from Armstrong, who tends not to deal in images like misty white clouds and *picture sounds of moving insects, so surreal.* The

familiar Armstrong theme of teenage angst/existential despair over the passage of time emerges on "16." The lyric to "I Was There," written by drummer John Kiffmeyer, takes a similar tone, leading one to wonder who was influencing whom during Green Day's formative years.

Kiffmeyer's small lyrical contribution certainly outshines his drumming on 39/Smooth, which is universally abysmal. His meters lurch all over the place almost comedically and drag the momentum of even the best songs. Coming out of a rhythmic change-up or one of his all-too-frequent sloppy snare rolls, he clearly struggles to reestablish the groove. Kiffmeyer's abdication of the Green Day drum throne, shortly after 39/Smooth was completed, was arguably his greatest contribution to the group's music.

On the up side, bands with weak or wild drummers often foster incredible bass players. Such is the case with Dirnt, whose nimble fret work and flawless vocal harmonies had already become an integral part of Green Day's sound by the time 39/Smooth was committed to tape. The close bond between Armstrong and Dirnt, both instrumentally and vocally, has always been central to the band's formidable power.

All told, there's something endearingly cute about these baby steps from a band destined to become a giant. Never meant to be a major blockbuster album, 39/Smooth was created for a cult audience—the Gilman Street/Maximumrockandroll '90s indie punk crowd. And in reissue packages that bundle it with early Green Day EPs, it will live on as a cult classic.

Nonetheless, the cumulative buzz in the punk subculture around the early EPs and *39/Smooth* was strong enough to allow Green Day to embark on their first tour, crisscrossing the country in an Econoline van. They hit the road the day Dirnt graduated from high school. This was spartan punk rock touring *par excellence*, driving vast distances overnight and building a following one sweaty venue at time. During a stop in Minneapolis, Armstrong met the young woman who would eventually become his wife.

A dreadlocked punk rocker with a fondness for thrift-store dresses, Adrienne Nesser was studying sociology at the University of Minnesota when she met Billie Joe at a Green Day gig. There was an instant affinity between the two, but their relationship would remain platonic and long-distance for a few years. The song "2,000 Light Years Away," expressing the loneliness of the long-distance lover, would be the first of many inspired by Nesser.

Shortly after returning from the tour, Armstrong and Erica Paleno broke up, although the two would remain friends. Billie Joe had a brief dalliance with a girl named Amanda, a militant punk rock feminist who ultimately jilted him. She became the subject of another massive Green Day hit, "Good Riddance (Time of Your Life)," and she inspired the character and song "Whatsername" along with "She's a Rebel" from *American Idiot*. But the breakups with Erica and Amanda weren't the only relationship changes in Billie Joe's life at the time. It was also shortly after their first tour that John Kiffmeyer announced he was leaving the band to pursue a college education. The first chapter of Green Day's career had come to an end. But the best was yet to come.

▼ The Playground, November 17, 1990. Shortly after Green Day's first tour, Kiffmeyer announced he was leaving the band to go to college. The move ended chapter one of the band's career—and made way for the man seated behind the kit here. Murray Bowles

chapter 3

ENTRÉ TRÉ COOL.

Drummers tend to come and go quite a bit in rock music. (Hence the telling fiction of Spinal Tap's foredoomed series of exploding trapsmen.) Yet the acquisition of just the right drummer is often the key determining factor in the success and core identity of any group. The Beatles weren't the Beatles until they got Ringo Starr (although Pete Best's mom might not agree). The Who weren't the Who until madcap Keith Moon jumped behind the kit one fateful night. And so it was with Green Day. The day they became the archetypal pop punk trio we know today was the day that a mercurial gentleman named Tré Cool joined their ranks.

   Much like the late Keith Moon, Cool is a bundle of crazy energy that turns to sheer magic when directed at a drum kit, but just as often finds expression in bizarre, elaborate, and generally off-color jokes. Compact yet solidly built, Tré possesses a rubbery, sad sack, working-class kind of face that seems tailor-made for comedy. And indeed, he attended classes to learn how to become a clown at one point. It was Lawrence Livermore who brought Cool to Green Day, which was something of a sacrifice, as the drummer had been playing with Livermore's own band, the Lookouts. Like many who meet the ebullient Mr. Cool for the first time, Armstrong and Dirnt had some reservations about his demonstrative personality, but ultimately accepted him as one of their own.

足を／兎を検査しましょう。

Frank Edwin Wright was born on December 9, 1972, in Willits, California, a rural Northern California town far more remote than Rodeo. Early on, he adopted the name Tré Cool, a corruption of the semi-French phrase *trés cool*, or very cool. He was a precocious and inquisitive kid with a hyperactive imagination.

"You know that kid who won't accept the fact that there's no genitals on a Barbie doll, or on dogs in cartoons?" Cool demanded. "I was that kid. 'How come that dog doesn't have a weenie like our dog?' I used to like the word weenie. Other kids just accepted it. They'd move on from there and watch the cartoon. Not me. If I don't see dicks and balls, I change the channel."

Cool was only twelve when he began drumming with the Lookouts and all of seventeen when he joined Green Day. He was a great fit on a number of levels. First and foremost, he was a markedly better drummer than Kiffmeyer, with just the right combination of speed, finesse, and manic energy to lift Armstrong's songcraft and the band's overall musicianship to a new level. Something of a power struggle developed between Kiffmeyer, as the eldest band member/de facto manager, and Armstrong, as the band's main songwriter/lead singer/frontman. No such issues arose with Cool, who was Armstrong's and Dirnt's peer, and whose unique way of asserting himself didn't encroach on Billie Joe's turf.

⋀ The rhythm section finds an easy cohesion at U-Gene's, Pico Rivera, January 26, 1991. Both Murray Bowles

GREEN DAY

1,039/Smoothed Out Slappy Hours

❮ Released on Lookout! in July 1991, *1,039/Smoothed Out Slappy Hours* compiled the band's debut LP and first two EPs.

924 Gilman Street, May 3, 1991.
Both Murray Bowles

Plus, Cool's whacked-out Huntz Hall persona brought an element of comic relief to Green Day's presentation. His antics provided an ideal foil for Armstrong's twitchy, but cute, adolescent angst and Dirnt's blue-collar intensity. Trios are a bit like three-legged stools. Each member has to carry more or less equal weight or the whole thing will fall down. Cool could hold up his end, both behind the kit and in photo shoots and interviews, albeit always with an inimitable flair all his own. Finally, Tré Cool made an ideal third member of Green Day because he shared Billie Joe and Mike's fondness for weed. Brotherhood in the bong is a bond that endures.

So it was a stronger, more unified Green Day that entered the studio in spring 1991 to record the band's second album, *Kerplunk*. Though Kiffmeyer, reluctant to let go completely, was still in the picture as a production advisor, the moment clearly belongs to Cool, Armstrong, and Dirnt. Released in January 1992, *Kerplunk* is a confident disc, arguably the first "proper" Green Day album. The tunes are better and the arrangements tighter than anything that had come before.

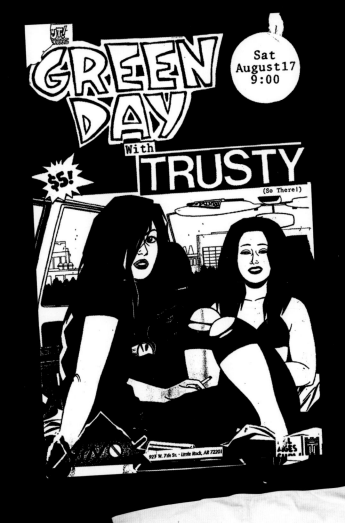

Flier for 1991 show at Vino's
in Little Rock, Arkansas.
Artist: Unknown

Early tour T-shirt.
AjcuVintage.com

Poster for show at Klub Ack, Bialystok, Poland, November 12, 1991, and blank poster for other Polish dates. The latter reads, "Melodic Punk, straight from the USA." Artist: Emil Hueso

January 1992

THE ALBUMS

Kerplunk

The low-budget, indie punk packaging of Green Day's second album belies the polished performances and well-conceived arrangements of the ten tracks therein. *Kerplunk* is the album on which Green Day really became *Green Day*. One can feel the adrenaline rush of self-discovery in every frenetic groove and precision guitar/bass/drums assault, all of which make the disc a great listen, even two decades down the road from its original release on Lookout! Records.

No small part of *Kerplunk* 's strength derives from the arrival of Tré Cool on the drummer's throne, replacing John Kiffmeyer, a.k.a. Al Sobrante. A far more competent and confident drummer than his predecessor, Cool brings not only the runaway libidinous energy necessary to propel the songs at warp speed, but also the discipline to bring Billie Joe Armstrong's and Mike Dirnt's well-honed guitar-and-bass arrangements into sharper focus. He punches where they punch, feints where they feint, and never misses a beat.

The real key to the album's success, however, is Billie Joe's uncanny ability to come up with one great melody after another. There's not one stinker in this stack of tunes. *Kerplunk* contains the all-time Green Day anthem, "Welcome to Paradise," which would become a worldwide mega hit when the band rerecorded the song for its major label release, *Dookie*, two years later, in 1994. This earlier version is virtually identical to the more well-known recording, right down to the breakdown section with its daunting bass line and atmospheric guitar overdubs, although the whole thing is played at a slightly more breakneck pace.

But "Welcome to Paradise" is just the tip of the iceberg. *Kerplunk* is awash in killer melodies, anthemic choruses, and virally in-fectious hooks. Ironically, however, all of this mature tunefulness is generally marshaled in service of trademark Billie Joe lyrics of post-adolescent angst and intimations of mortality. "Who Wrote Holden Caufield?" even refer-ences the protagonist in *Catcher in the Rye*, J. D. Salinger's American lit classic of youth-ful alienation. The track's "never mind" refrain even echoes Kurt Cobain's epoch-defining grunge gloom. (The release of Nirvana's *Nevermind* preceded that of *Kerplunk* by only a few months.)

Leave it to Tré Cool to lighten the mood—sort of—with his country-and-western bondage song, "Dominated Love Slave," the first of Cool's several public declarations of his fascination with S&M. And, here on just the second Green Day album, we can hear Armstrong pull away from the songwriting constraints of up-tempo pop punk. With its old-school chord progression, "Christie Road" is more like an update on the Ramones's take on Phil Spector melodrama than anything coming out of Gilman Street at the time. And, following an arpeggiated bass intro that can only be described as lovely, "No One Knows" moves into a chordal and melodic pattern that wouldn't be out of place on an early Beatles ballad.

While Green Day would soon be excoriated by some for deserting Lookout! in favor of a major label deal, *Kerplunk* is the sound of a band bursting out of the constraints of the lo-fi indie punk ethos. You can hear the band's hunger to take on the whole wide world.

The *Kerplunk* packaging typifies the low-budget, indie-punk, Lookout! Records aesthetic in art direction (although the inner sleeve's handwritten lyrics, enclosed in rough-hewn borders, would set the pace for *Dookie*'s graphics after Green Day signed to Warner Bros.). *Kerplunk*'s liner notes include a satirical prose narrative, purportedly by a teenage Green Day fan named Laurie L., a student at Armstrong and Dirnt's real-life alma mater, Pinole Valley High School. In a breezy, offhand tone, she gleefully recounts how she fatally poisoned her parents in order to claim her prize in a "Win a Dream Date with Green Day" contest in the teen fan mag *Tiger Beat*. Even inevitable incarceration for the deed doesn't trouble her; the prison guards still let her listen to her Green Day tapes.

Like Sub Pop to the north, Lookout! Records was an outgrowth of a popular local 'zine. Published by Lawrence Livermore, the summer 1991 *Lookout!* featured a satirical teen mag-style "My Adventure with Billie Joe" essay that was included in *Kerplunk*'s liner notes.

GREEN DAY

WHY NOT GO CHECK THEIR FIRST TWO ALBUMS OUT MR. SMARTY PANTS?

HEY THINK YOU LOVE THOSE BOYS LIKE I LOVE THOSE BOYS?

LOOKOUT 22 "39/SMOOTH"

ON VINYL CASSETTE AND COMPACT DISC

LOOKOUT 46 "KERPLUNK!"

ONLY ON LOOKOUT RECORDS

LIKE MY TATTOO?

Lookout! retailer poster, 1992.

◄ This bootleg 7-inch–"put out by fans for fans," according to the back of the sleeve–was recorded August 28, 1992, and features "Long View," [sic] "Better Not Come Around," and "Don't Leave Me."

The piece pokes fun at the teen idol image that had become something of an embarrassment to Green Day even at this early stage in their career. It also sheds a sly light on the pervy side of the band's newest member, Tré Cool. "When I asked him for his autograph," writes Miss L., "he said I had to talk to his agent; and when I asked him who his agent was, he started to unzip his pants."

Kerplunk's music is considerably more mature than its packaging. The well-built arrangements are the sort that emerge only after a group plays together constantly, both in the rehearsal room and before audiences—tight, without being fussy or overcooked. Cool provided a newfound sense of easygoing cohesion, and Billie Joe's songwriting had grown considerably, enabling him to incorporate new melodic, harmonic, and structural ideas without seeming awkward or self-important. And Dirnt just seems to get better on every track.

"I think Mike's bass playing adds a second melody to the structure of our songs," Billie Joe noted. "There's two melodies going on. One is what I'm singing, the other is what Mike is playing on bass."

Lyrically, *Kerplunk* is very much a document of Billie Joe's stage in life at the time—just a few steps down the road from adolescence, but no less insecure, confronting the identity crises and romantic entanglements of early manhood. The album opens with "2,000 Light Years Away," Armstrong's forlorn declaration of longing for the absent Adrienne. Given Billie Joe's somewhat obsessive command of rock history, the allusion to the Rolling Stones' psychedelic-era track "2000 Light Years from Home" was probably deliberate.

Elsewhere, the songs skew between two distinct moods. On the one hand, there's a defiant sense of independence and jubilation at having found a place in the world after leaving home. On the other hand, several songs carry a mood of what can perhaps best be described as existential despair.

Notable among the album's triumphant, if dark, declarations of independence is "Welcome to Paradise," the song that Billie Joe had written in a Berkeley punk squat shortly after leaving the parental nest. It would become one of Green Day's biggest hits ever when rerecorded and rereleased as part of the band's third album, *Dookie*. The song has a special resonance for anyone who has ever found a safe haven behind the rough exterior of an outsider scene such as punk. No doubt, this is a factor in its enduring popularity.

In a similar vein, "Christie Road" references another Berkeley-area locale. Standing on the roof of his beat-up car, viewing distant hills at sunset and having smoked a joint, the singer says, *Now I feel like me once again.* The song's sense of newfound independence and uneasy freedom closely parallels "Welcome to Paradise."

Kerplunk is also long on evocations of the open road and its freedoms. The song "80" alludes to Interstate 80, one of the Bay Area's main freeways, here seen as a route of escape from anxiety, frustration, and romantic disillusionment.

Other songs deal in the kind of philosophical angst that ranks high among Armstrong's key lyrical themes. "Android" confronts the grim inevitabilities of aging and death—eventualities quite vivid, no doubt, to a young man who'd lost his father at the age of ten. Another of the album's tracks, "One of My Lies," asks the musical question *Why does my life have to be so small?/Yet death is forever/And does forever have a life to call its own*?

One might have higher expectations of finding lines like this in the work of Sartré or Kierkegaard than in a pop punk song. Armstrong goes so far as to reference J. D. Salinger's popular novel of alienated youth, *Catcher in the Rye*, in the song "Who Wrote Holden Caufield?," finding himself in much the same frustrated state as Salinger's protagonist. Coincidentally, the tune's *Oh well . . . Never mind* chorus tag line echoed what had the previous fall become the dismissive motto of disaffected, alienated '90s youth who eagerly adopted the title of Nirvana's major label breakthrough album, *Nevermind*.

The unrelenting gloom of some of Armstrong's lyrics on *Kerplunk* and elsewhere might be insufferable were they not married to some of the most infectious pop punk tunes ever penned. Green Day would exploit this tension between lyrics and music to great effect throughout their career.

While *Kerplunk* is competently recorded, it was becoming clear that Green Day were starting to outgrow the facilities at Berkeley's Art of Ears studio, where they'd recorded their first two albums, not to mention the resources of Lookout! Records. A simple comparison of the *Kerplunk* and *Dookie* versions of "Welcome to Paradise" offers convincing testimony as to how much more sonic depth and punch could be pulled from the three-piece juggernaut that Green Day had become, given a larger budget and a state-of-the-art studio.

Green Day were ready to move on. And soon they would do just that.

Artist: Adam Swinbourne/adamswinbourne.com

▲ From the start, Cool's unique way of asserting himself didn't encroach on Billie Joe's turf.
Murray Bowles

chapter **4**

TO THE MAJORS!

With two successful indie albums under their collective belt, each selling around 30,000 copies, Green Day were ripe for plucking by the major record labels. They'd already taken a step in this direction by abandoning Kiffmeyer-style self-management in favor of professional representation by the L.A.-based team of Elliot Kahn and Jeff Salzman. A move from the indies to the majors had long been the standard career trajectory for up-and-coming bands. And the phenomenal success that Geffen Records had garnered in the early '90s by signing Nirvana away from Seattle indie Sub Pop had created renewed interest on the part of the big labels in edgy sounds from music scenes in cities other than the music biz capitals of New York and L.A.

The Seattle grunge bands had all referenced punk rock with great reverence. But not one of them actually sounded very much like the Pistols, Damned, or Ramones. Meanwhile the hair-metal phenomenon of the '80s had all but obliterated punk's first wave, as far as the collective consciousness of mainstream rock consumers went. So maybe it was time for a full-scale punk rock revival.

On the verge of their big
breakthrough, February 1993.
John Popplewell/Retna Ltd.

△ SOMA, San Diego, 1993. Soon
the band would be headlining
arenas in markets where
previously they had played clubs.

▽ Green Day contributed a live
version of "Christy Road" to this
double 7-inch released by the
U.K.'s Fierce Panda label in 1994.

The man who overcame Green Day's Gilman Street reluctance to sign a major label
record contract was Rob Cavallo, a staff A&R man at Warner Bros./Reprise Records.
Under the leadership of Mo Ostin and Lenny Waronker, Warners had acquired a reputation
as an artist-friendly label. And their sublabel imprint, Sire, had been home to key first-wave
punk bands, such as the Ramones and Blondie.

But what really clinched the deal was when Cavallo flew up to the Bay Area to visit Green
Day in their rehearsal space. He ended up strapping on a guitar, sharing a few joints with the
band, and jamming with the group. By some accounts, it was Cavallo's knowledge of Beatles
chord progressions that won Billie Joe over. The guy was clearly no corporate suit, and
Cavallo would have an important role in shaping Green Day's sound over the coming years as
their producer.

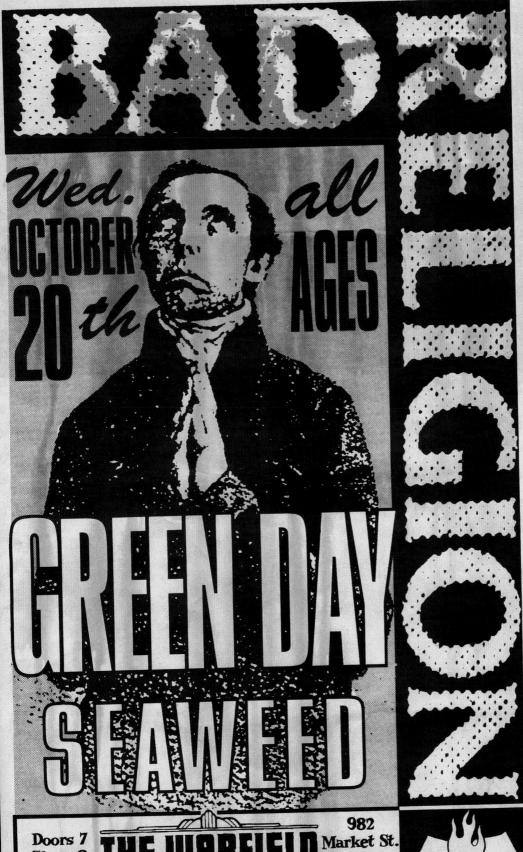

BAD RELIGION

Wed.
OCTOBER
20th

all
AGES

GREEN DAY
SEAWEED

Doors 7
Show 8

THE WARFIELD

982
Market St.
S.F.

TICKETS AT BASS, INCLUDING WHEREHOUSE & TOWER RECORDS INFO:(415) 775-7722

▲ Sauntering the streets of
Manhattan, early 1994. Ken Schles/
Time Life Pictures/Getty Images

In late 1993, Cavallo brought Green Day into Berkeley's Fantasy Studio, which had been one of the Bay Area's leading recording facilities since the 1960s. With better technical facilities and a larger budget than they'd enjoyed for either of their Lookout! albums, Green Day were able to deepen, broaden, and fine-tune their sound and overall attack, bringing Billie Joe's incisive and often cleverly self-deprecating songs into sharper focus than ever.

The resulting album appeared on February 1, 1994, bearing the title *Dookie*, a juvenile appellation for feces. It takes considerable nerve to put out an album called, in essence, *Shit*. But Green Day's unique brand of adolescent, self-denigrating humor was something that made them instantly appealing when *Dookie* was released. Critics and journalists invariably, and gleefully, described them as "bratty." And when Nirvana's Kurt Cobain took his own life with a shotgun on April 5, 1994, just four months after *Dookie*'s release, "bratty" suddenly seemed to offer a much-welcome respite from the unremitting gloom of the grunge movement Cobain had spearheaded, and of grunge's U.K. cousins, the "shoe-gazer" bands.

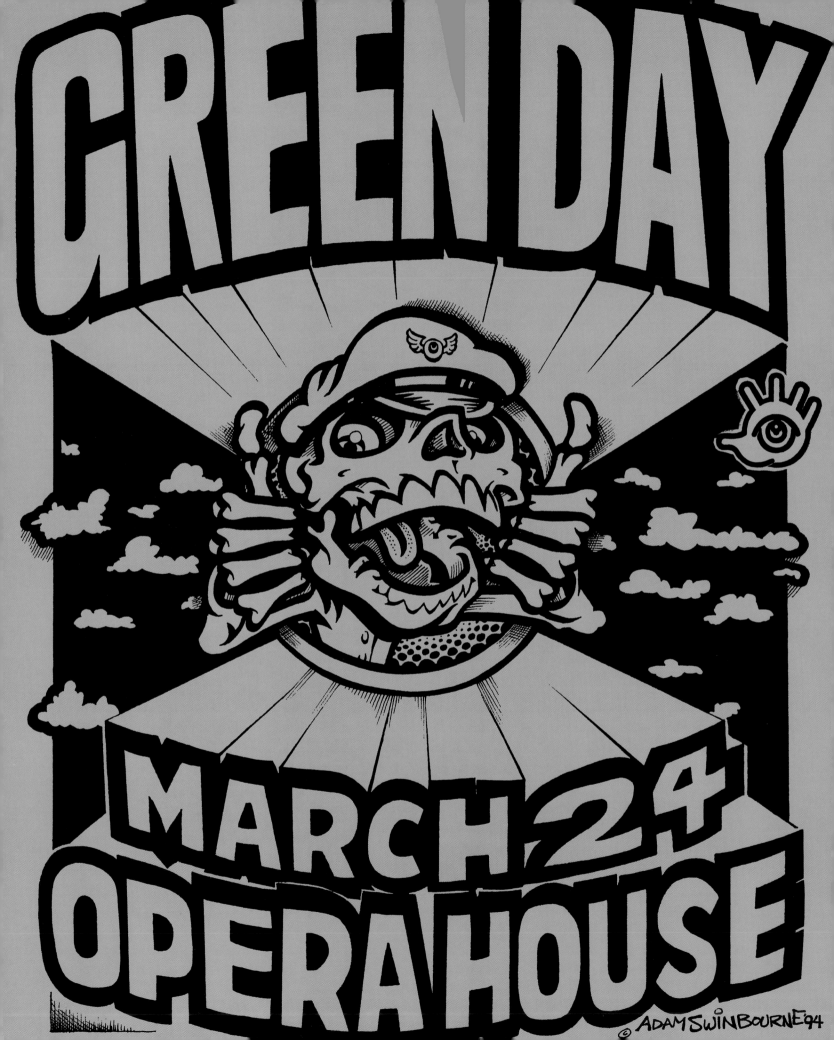

At the legendary First Avenue club in Adrienne's hometown of Minneapolis on March 29, 1994, just a few months before she and Billie Joe wed. Both Jim Steinfeldt/Michael Ochs Archives/ Getty Images

> The major label debut that launched a legion of loud, fast, three-chord bands with tuneful lead vocals.

February 1994

THE ALBUMS

Dookie

The pop punk revolution starts here. Green Day's 1994 major label debut is the disc that launched a legion of loud, fast, three-chord bands with nasal, if tuneful, lead vocals. Many of these have since fallen by the wayside—most of them deservedly so. But *Dookie* still stands today as a sustained rush of pure pop punk bliss.

On Green Day's third album, Billie Joe Armstrong seems far from exhausting what appears to be a boundless capacity for creating crisp, bright vocal melodies that sound completely fresh—and yet, even on a first listen, also hauntingly familiar. They're designed to become your favorite songs from the instant they hit you over the head—and to stay that way.

Dookie was, and remains, the clarion call for a new breed of disaffected youth. From the opening salvo of "Burnout" to the snickering fizzle-out of the hidden track, "All by Myself," *Dookie* explores the classic punk themes of boredom, alienation, futility, wasted time, self-loathing, psychotherapy

and dysfunctional romance, but from a fresh and snidely clever perspective. The legacy of the Ramones looms large, although not exclusively.

Combining two popular rock song themes, the massive hit "Longview" ponders the concept of masturbating out of boredom. "Having a Blast," which explores the cultivated indifference of a suicide bomber, could be a '90's rewrite of Fear's punk classic "I Don't Care About You." And it manages to sound even more brutalized and dispassionate than its predecessor.

In *Dookie*'s fourteen songs, we meet a rogues' gallery of misfits, dorks, and creeps, most of whom somehow resemble Billie Joe himself. These characterizations are drawn with just a few deft strokes. Most songs possess no more than two verses, which are repeated just the right number of times. *Dookie* is a masterpiece of spare economy. Armstrong, Mike Dirnt, and Tré Cool have clearly worked out every twist and turn in the dynamic trigonometry of a three-piece rock band.

"She" is one of several tracks that withhold the entry of sledgehammer guitars for maximum impact. Songs screech to a blinding halt to make way for dizzying bass fillips and berserk drum breaks with unerring musical logic.

And although the pace is unrelenting, Armstrong and company know how to create both rhythmic and melodic variety. "When I Come Around" abandons the breakneck pace of the other songs in favor of a menacing mid-tempo lurch. Billie Joe's "love hurts" song, "Pulling Teeth," has the melodic lilt of an old-school R&B hit. One can almost imagine Sam Cooke singing that melody—had Sam Cooke been born in the '70s with a safety pin through his nose.

All told, *Dookie* is an irresistible invitation to join a happy throng of outsider fuckups, ready to follow Green Day to the ends of the earth. Not a bad place to spend the '90s—or the rest of one's life.

Interestingly, *Dookie* songs like "Burnout" and "Longview" dwell on much the same adolescent feelings of boredom, low self-esteem, and listless futility as Nirvana's "Smells Like Teen Spirit" and Radiohead's "Creep." But Green Day's touch is much lighter. For all the dark undertones of a song like "Having a Blast," which deals with a suicide bomber, the mood is essentially comedic. This tone was underscored by the goofball cartoon illustrations that adorned *Dookie*'s lyric sheet and seemed like a direct riff on John Holmstrom's comic illustrations for the Ramones' *Rocket to Russia*. Rather than wallowing in the isolation of being an outsider, Dookie presents a winning case that it's kinda cool to be a reject.

"Basically what we are is a rock and roll band," Billie Joe said at the time. "We're way more extroverted and exhibitionist types. We're not shoe gazers. No way. We're demented. I'm gonna take my fuckin' clothes off and wiggle my little dick in front of everybody. I'm gonna be totally obnoxious and rude and spit in the eye of every fucking heavy grunge band that ever came out. Not that we wanted to become the next big thing after grunge."

"Still," Dirnt added, "it's nice that people actually picked out a difference between us and some of the grunge stuff. I really like Nirvana, but there's really a difference between them and us. There's melodic song structure in both, but musically there's a lot of difference. It's weird that people were able to pick out that difference. I thought a lot of people would just throw it all in the same class."

The Dookie campaign featured illustrations by East Bay artist and musician Richie Bucher. WycoVintage.com

Billie Joe consults his setlist at Live 105's BFD, June 10, 1994. © Jay Blakesberg/Corbis

1yoVintage.com

Live 105's BFD, Shoreline
Amphitheatre, Mountain View,
California, June 10, 1994. Tim
Mosenfelder/Getty Images

▼ "Basket Case" b/w "2,000 Light Years Away," limited edition green vinyl for the U.K.

Dookie yielded a string of massive hits that made Green Day one of the biggest rock acts in 1994 and 1995. First out of the box was "Longview," remarkable for Mike Dirnt's walking bass line—a playing style not often heard in punk rock—and lyrics that ponder the pros and cons of masturbation. It was followed by "Welcome to Paradise," Billie Joe's back-catalog song about a punk rock squat that first appeared on *Kerplunk*. The *Dookie* version illustrates just how far Green Day had come in the two or so years since *Kerplunk*. While the arrangement is essentially the same, the *Dookie* performances, Cool's in particular, are appreciably tighter. Reaping the benefits of a first-rate studio, the sound is appreciably fatter and meaner.

Green Day's assault on the charts continued with "Basket Case," boasting the memorable hook line *sometimes I give myself the creeps*. "When I Come Around" broke into the U.S. Top 10 and was followed by "She." The anguished protagonist of "She" foreshadows some of the female characters Billie Joe would create on *American Idiot* and *21st Century Breakdown* a few years later.

Tré Cool's songwriting contribution to *Dookie* was the hidden bonus track "All by Myself," while Dirnt wrote the lyric to "Emenis Sleepus." The accident-prone bassist also provided the subject matter for "Pulling Teeth."

"My wife accidentally broke both my arms," Dirnt explained. "We had a pillow fight. I was running from her and ran into a horizontal beam."

Dirnt incurred further injury at Green Day's historic appearance at the Woodstock '94 festival in August of that year. Commemorating the twenty-fifth anniversary of the original Woodstock festival, perhaps the only thing that the '94 Woodstock had in common with its peace-and-love predecessor was horrid weather. History repeated itself as a torrential downpour reduced the festival grounds to a slippery, slimy field of mud. Green Day seized the moment by provoking a massive mud fight with the audience, making worldwide headlines and turning their set into one of the most talked-about performances of the entire festival.

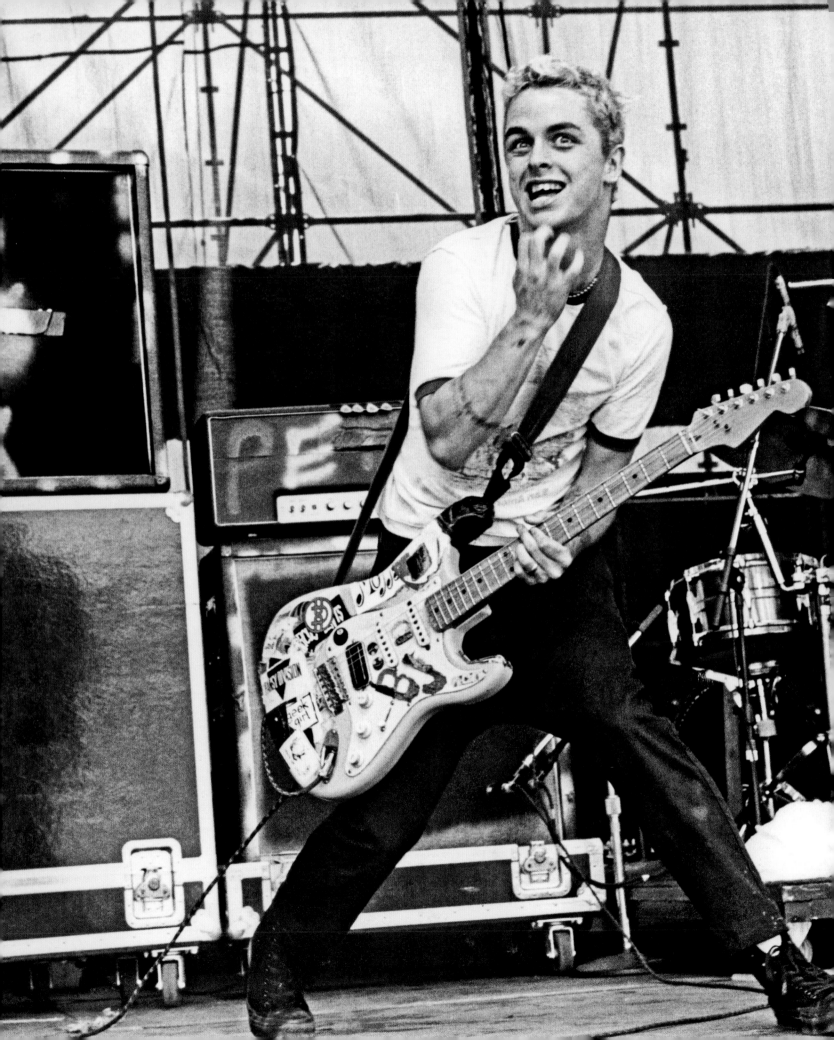

Lollapalooza, Downing Stadium, Randall's Island Park, New York, August 2004. Ebet Roberts/ Redferns/Getty Images

Warner Bros. commissioned this poster to help promote the bands from its labels that appeared on the 1994 Lollapalooza tour. Artist: Dwight Mackintosh/ creativegrowth.org

But in the fracas, Dirnt took a beating from a security goon. "I lost teeth during that incident," the bassist recalled. "Some security guard thought I was a crowd kid and dove and tackled me. I suppose it's better it was me rather than some kid in the crowd, because I was able to get out and get to a dentist. 'Cause the guy broke three of my bottom teeth and scraped all the rest of them to shit. . . . I had one root canal done the next day. I sat in the dentist's office for eight hours getting all the drilling done. It sucked, man. It was so much pain . . . if I had it to do all over again, I'd get my guitar and knock that guard's ass out."

Armstrong did jump on the guard's back and mete out some retribution for Dirnt's suffering. "I punched him quite a few times," Billie Joe confirmed. "I don't know if it had much effect on him. He was quite a big guy."

"No, you did," Dirnt replied. "My friend tried to talk to the guy afterwards and he was holding himself up."

▲ Woodstock '94, before
the mud—and the dental work—
Saugerties, New York, August 14,
1994. AP Photo/Robert F. Bukaty

Just as the original Woodstock played a key role in launching the careers of major rock acts, such as Santana, Mountain, and Crosby, Stills & Nash, Woodstock '94 confirmed Green Day's arrival as a significant new force in rock music. None of which sat very well with the band's original indie punk fan base. It was bad enough that Green Day had violated the Gilman ban on signing with a major label, but then they'd had the further effrontery to go multiplatinum. Disaffected punk picketers outside of some Green Day shows carried placards and shouted abuse. The band was denounced from the pages of *Maximumrockandroll* with Stalinist rigor. It was painful to be rejected by their former peers and the scene that had nurtured them, but Armstrong, Dirnt, and Cool had a larger musical destiny to fulfill.

> The massive success of *Dookie* saw Green Day graduating to basketball arenas in cities where little more than a year prior they were headlining clubs with a $6 cover charge.

∨ Backstage pass, Expo Park, Tampa, Florida, 1994.

"I don't set any rules on myself," Billie Joe said. "I don't live up to anybody's expectations. I'm totally self-sufficient. That's what punk is more about to me. Not creating this elitist attitude. I'm not elitist at all. I have all different kinds of friends. I'm into all different strange people and different lifestyles. Even if someone was a Republican, I could still find some way to get along with them—sit down, have a discussion, and talk about life. I think that elitist *Maximumrockandroll* punks are a lot more conservative than Republicans."

Meanwhile, Green Day drew the contempt from some members of punk's old guard, who felt that the Berkeley upstarts had trivialized the genre. Green Day were also charged with being derivative of pop-minded late-'70s punk bands, such as the Buzzcocks and the Dickies.

"We always get this thing about how we're trying to sound like the Buzzcocks," Dirnt complained. "But I hadn't even heard the fucking Buzzcocks when we started!"

SPECIAL GUESTS

PANSY DIVISION
DIE TOTEN HOSEN
Thursday, Dec 1 · 8pm

Presented by

Electric Factory Concerts

(215) 336-2000

PHILADELPHIA CIVIC CENTER
34th & Civic Center Blvd.

There was even a public pissing match with Johnny Rotten, who infamously called Green Day "plonk not punk." "I love the Sex Pistols' old songs," said Armstrong. "I think the lyrics are really great. And I really like Johnny Rotten's book a lot [*Rotten: No Irish, No Blacks, No Dogs*]. But now he sounds like my grandmother at times. He sounds old. And that's the funny thing. He's so predictable in his comments about us. I mean, come on, be a bit more novel. . . . On top of that, some of the stuff from PiL was complete shit, as far as I'm concerned."

But while Green Day alienated some, they drew a massive new audience. *Dookie* would ultimately go fifteen times platinum (and counting) and be a key factor in igniting the pop punk explosion that would become a predominant voice in '90s rock. But in time, *Dookie* also would become something of an albatross around Green Day's neck—some people expected every subsequent Green Day album to sound the same and sell just as many copies. But Green Day were never ones to repeat a formula just to score hit records. As a result, it would take the band a full decade to top the success of their major-label debut.

◄ San Francisco "queercore" band Pansy Division opened several dates on the *Dookie* tour.

➤ The band left Lookout! on friendly terms, though this treatment of the *Kerplunk* flower, circa 1994, would suggest otherwise. WycoVintage.com

PANIC ATTACKS AND INSOMNIACS

Dookie changed the lives of Armstrong, Dirnt, and Cool in many ways. Financially secure for the first time since leaving home, they strove to establish stable and secure domestic lives amid the insanity of rock stardom. Billie Joe and Adrienne married in 1994. Their first child, Joseph Marciano Armstrong, arrived on February 28, 1995. Dirnt had married his first wife, Anastasia. Tré Cool wed Lisa Lyons, who gave birth to the couple's first child, Ramona, in January 1995. All three newlywed couples bought homes in the Bay Area.

But domestic bliss has never been entirely compatible with the rock 'n' roll lifestyle. Asked, around that time, if parenthood slows one down, Billie Joe responded, "What doesn't kill you will make you stronger. That's all I've got to say about that."

The transition from careless youth to marriage and parenthood is a big adjustment for anyone. But at the same time, the members of Green Day had to deal with the rigors that go with being a highly successful musical act riding out the first rush of fame. They maintained a relentless touring schedule as *Dookie*'s momentum refused to slow down throughout 1994 and much of '95. There was the standard rock star weirdness of not being able to walk around their own neighborhoods anymore and being treated oddly by old friends and family. Added to this, Green Day bore the odd double burden of being vilified as sellouts by some while being adored by others.

> Sick of the road and still a few years out from successfully experimenting with the form and format of rock songs, December 1995. Jay Blakesberg/blakesberg.com

All of these situations were reflected on Green Day's follow-up to *Dookie*, 1995's much-anticipated *Insomniac*. Harder sounding than *Dookie*, it is very much an album of identity crisis. Who were Green Day? Armstrong, Dirnt, and Cool themselves weren't quite sure.

"When we made *Dookie* we were more lower-middle class," Armstrong said. "Maybe a lot of what's going on in *Insomniac* is that struggle to keep it there. Keep it together and still convey that we're a working-class band."

Once again, Rob Cavallo was at the production helm. *Insomniac* was recorded at Hyde Street studios in San Francisco and at Ocean Way in L.A. The latter studio would be the birthplace of many more Green Day albums to come. Part of *Insomniac*'s harder edged sound, compared with *Dookie*, is down to Cavallo's suggestion to have electronics wiz Bob Bradshaw turbocharge the band's amps. "Rob knows Bob Bradshaw, who's a hot rod amplifier guy," Billie Joe said, "We took a couple of Marshall amplifier heads and speaker cabinets and turned them up full blast. For *Insomniac*, we wanted to come up with a sound that was totally saturated."

This limited-edition U.K. 7-inch picture disc featured "When I Come Around" b/w "She" recorded live at the Aragon Ballroom in Chicago on November 18, 1994.

< The *Berkley Blockbuster* 7-inch bootleg featured Green Day's December 3, 1994, *Saturday Night Live* performances of "When I Come Around" and "I Dunno" (a.k.a. "Geek Stink Breath").

The main stage at Reading '95 featured a veritable who's who of former indie-rock darlings that the major labels had jockeyed to sign in the post-Nirvana boom.

> CD single sleeve for Billie Joe's ode to methamphetamine-induced halitosis. The disc also featured the previously unreleased "I Want to Be on TV" and "Don't Want to Fall in Love."

"I think the recording of it is more like you're standing in our practice room," said Dirnt. "When we practice, we face all our instruments toward each other and just pound as loud as we can. That's how the mix of *Insomniac* sounds to me. It's a lot less polished than *Dookie*."

The album title refers to the sleepless nights that Billie Joe and Adrienne endured tending to their infant son. But touring with a rock band is another very effective way not to get enough sleep. Feelings of disorientation and panic are known byproducts of sleep deprivation, and this is the predominant mood of *Insomniac*. Tracks like "Panic Song," "Brain Stew," "Armatage Shanks," "Walking Contradiction," and "Geek Stink Breath" all speak in one way or another of being trapped inside a troubled mind and, often, seeking to escape ones' own self through self-destructive behavior. Billie Joe is particularly hard on himself in "Geek Stink Breath," which alludes to his earlier flirtation with methamphetamine, which is known to dry the mouth, causing halitosis. Hence the title.

"'Geek Stink Breath' is autobiographical," he admitted. "Whereas 'Basket Case' [from *Dookie*] was about someone else. That's more of a character. For the lyrics to *Insomniac*, I wanted to take things line by line. I really concentrated on a lot of the lyrics. I really thought about things a lot. I think the mood of *Insomniac* is completely different from *Dookie*. For me, lyrically, it's just a gloomier record. It's got a lot of mood swings to it. *Dookie* was the action and *Insomniac* was the reaction."

With its dark lyrics and edgier guitar sound, *Insomniac* seems like a deliberate push away from the top of the charts. But, even from this grim material, Armstrong couldn't help but create incredibly catchy pop songs. "Geek Stink Breath" became the successful first single release from *Insomniac*, in spite of a disturbing video clip that included graphic and bloody clinical footage of a dental extraction. MTV refused to air the clip during the day, but it became a favorite on the network's late-night alternative rock show *120 Minutes*.

However, *Insomniac* isn't entirely focused on introspective self-loathing. Billie Joe's knack for social commentary and arch characterization comes to fore on "Brat." Given the autobiographical tone of so many other songs on *Insomniac*, some listeners mistook the song's spoiled, rich kid protagonist for another self-portrait—Billie Joe, the pampered, wealthy rock star. Armstrong found this misinterpretation particularly annoying.

"'Brat' is very much about the UC Berkeley college student," he clarified. "The new college students come in and they'd see Telegraph Street [Berkeley's main thoroughfare], with all the tie-die shirts everywhere and go, 'Wow I really am in the land of the free. Thank God mom and dad are paying the rent.'"

Berkeley students of the "Brat" variety were universally held in contempt by the Gilman Street punk crowd. But *Insomniac* also contains a heartfelt kiss-off to Gilman Street in the song, "86." The song is Armstrong's own personal "Don't Look Back," born of the realization that he and the band had reached a point of no return. Rejection by Gilman hardliners had been painful, but Green Day had their own road to travel and a growing musical vision far broader than Gilman Street's punk purist perspective.

"Hey, don't blame me for the [pop] punk rock explosion," Dirnt said. "I didn't know our music was going to get that big. Anyway, we deliberately removed ourselves from the punk rock scene because the wrong elements were coming into the scene, and we were just getting too big for it anyway."

"In a lot of ways, *Insomniac* was a step back, as far as writing pop songs," Billie Joe reflected. "We limited ourselves and broke things down even more. But now we've got this foundation; we can go anywhere we want. I want to go anywhere I can in writing the three-minute, catchy song. You can experiment with the three-minute song without becoming 'experimental.' There's so much you could achieve. The thought has crossed my mind to make the next one a double album."

‹ Promotional stickers for *Insomniac*.

Brixton Academy, London,
September 20, 1995. Fred Duval/
FilmMagic/Getty Images

Green Day
Insomniac

October 1995

THE ALBUMS

Insomniac

The gloomiest Green Day album ever? *Insomniac* may well claim that distinction.

Of course, gloom is a relative term. Compared with a recording by, say, Joy Division or Cannibal Corpse, *Insomniac* is an outright tune fest. Still, one can clearly hear how the strain of rock stardom took its toll on Billie Joe Armstrong, Mike Dirnt, and Tré Cool in the aftermath of *Dookie*'s massive mid-'90s success. The follow-up to *Dookie*, *Insomiac* is the former album's dark doppelganger. It's the hangover that inevitably follows an excess of anything, even fame.

An element of self-contempt had always been present in Armstrong's writing. But here he brings it on relentlessly, beginning with the opening track, "Armitage Shanks," in which the singer comes right out and declares himself a "self-loathing freak."

The overall sound of *Insomniac* is also fittingly darker than anything Green Day had done before. The guitars are gutsier and

They claw and scratch savagely. The drum sound is more live, thudding relentlessly with a kind of plucky, rehearsal hall desperation.

All this grim stuff is projected with little or none of the redeeming humor and comic relief of Green Day's earlier albums. Nor are there any songs of romance, not even the dysfunctional variety, on *Insomniac*. The whole thing is pretty much one sustained public act of self-laceration on Billie Joe's part, exacerbated by an apparent bout of methamphetimene abuse.

"Geek Stink Breath" is a blatant confession of drug-induced helplessness. "Brain Stew" chugs along at a narcotized, "Kashmir" pace, its scratchy rhythm guitar aurally evoking the dry mouth and skin itches that meth brings on. Billie Joe's rapid-fire vocal delivery over the stop-and-go guitar chording of "Bab's Uvula Who?" is pure wound-up, tweaked-out speed-freak intensity. But perhaps the album's most brilliant sonic evocation of amphetamine overkill is Mike Dirnt's manic

double-picked, one-note bass intro in the aptly titled "Panic Song." An act of superhuman endurance, the performance must have had his wrist hurting for weeks.

Which is a key point. While many songs on *Insomniac* deftly dramatize what it's like to be fucked up on speed, the performances exhibit a flawless self-possession and command that no real, hardcore druggie can claim. And while Billie Joe's melodic muse seems to desert him at times on *Insomniac*— on the Gilman street kiss-off song "86" for instance—there are also moments when his winning way with a tune bursts through. Such is the case on the closing track, "Walking Contradiction," in spite of lyrics that proclaim still more personal nihilism. But then the song *is* called "Walking Contradiction."

The dark side is often the abode of great art, and *Insomniac* is no exception. While not as instantly rousing or pop bliss–inducing as other Green Day albums, it's well worth

Circa 1995 tour shirts.
All WycoVintage.com

It would be a few more years, and a few more albums in the can, before Armstrong would create a large-scale album that experimented, successfully, with the form and format of rock songs. For the moment, once *Insomniac* was completed, the band had to buckle down to another round of international touring. This was a particularly daunting prospect, as Green Day had never fully recovered from the *Dookie* tour.

"We never got to take a break," said Dirnt. "After [*Dookie*], we said, 'Okay, we're taking eight months off.' But Billie and Tré both had kids, which is not time off. No way. And during that time, Billie was writing like crazy and we were in our rehearsal room every day, practicing our asses off. Then we went right in the studio for a few months and then right out on the road again."

Touring began to take a physical as well as psychological toll on Dirnt, in particular. His knees and ankles began to hurt constantly from jumping around on stage night after night. But far worse was a mysterious chest pain that he feared indicated a serious heart condition.

"I feel like I'm having minor heart attacks all the time," he said. "My doctors thought it was a microvalve prolapse, but that wasn't what it was. I've had EKGs and stuff. I'm at the point now where I'm sick of looking for it. If it kills me, it kills me. It's been happening for a long time now. But it's just gotten worse. Basically, I'm standing there and all of a sudden it'll be like somebody jams a syringe needle in my chest. I drop to the ground gasping. And then my heart's always sore. It's a scary thing to have with the one part of your body that they don't know how to fix."

Dirnt's problem would turn out to be a far less serious gastric condition. But it was years before he received a definitive diagnosis. Meanwhile, his worries about his health were taking it out of him on the road.

"I was having panic attacks every day," he said. "Basically the doctors wanted me on Xanax or Prozac or that shit all the time. And I wasn't gonna do it. I'd take a Xanax when I got so physically nauseous I couldn't go on stage. And sometimes I would pass out. I'd say, 'Oh God, I gotta lie down.' Then I'd wake up six hours later—just from exhaustion."

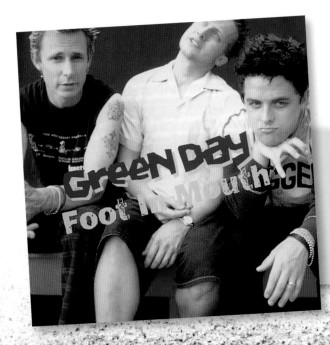

Green Day offered their first live releases just months apart, in April and July 1996. *Foot in Mouth* featured eleven tracks recorded on the *Dookie* and *Insomniac* tours. *Bowling . . .* was a seven-track EP brought out in Japan, Europe, and South America only.

Nor were Dirnt's band mates very happy on the road. "Playing those huge arenas really sucked," Armstrong said after the *Insomniac* tour. "I tried to be optimistic about it, but it just sucked. That's not our thing. We're a three-piece, tight-knit band, and we belong in a tight-knit room. I think we belong in theaters. Theaters have so much more class and they're meant for playing music. It's not where the fucking Chicago Bulls or the Oakland A's play. That's not what our music is about. We're more into relating to the audience at eye level and not becoming these huge monsters of rock for people."

Matters came to a head when the tour hit the big sheds of Europe. "Before that, we did a tour of Asia and the shows were much smaller, from 1,200 to 2,500 people," Dirnt explained. "And we had a great time. We were way tighter; came across way better. When you're all right next to each other, jumping in the air, bumping into each other in midair, falling all over each other, it's so much better. When you can hear the actual instruments playing from each other's amps, instead of some mix coming out of the monitors, it's a way more intense feeling. We all get a better reaction off each other; the crowd gets a better reaction and everything. But then going out and doing Europe again, after that, it just seemed like homework."

"It was a slap of reality," Billie Joe added. "Why are we so miserable? Oh, because we like playing small places better than these big places."

And so Green Day decided to cancel their tour midway through Europe. It was a difficult choice. But for the band, it was a matter of getting their priorities straight.

"I'd always sacrificed Adrienne and Joey for the band," Armstrong said. "But I wanted to prove something to her, like, 'Now I'm gonna sacrifice the band for you. Because you come first, before anyone else.' I felt like I wasn't being an attentive parent. And Joey's now at an age. . . . The first three years are really the most important. These years will really shape his whole identity and personality. How could I miss those? And plus my wife is way overworked being a parent. I just had no reason to be on the road and every reason to come home."

"This is the first time we put ourselves above the crowd or above our music in any way whatsoever," Dirnt said. "But we felt if we want to extend this, keep on making music and exist as people and a band, we just gotta take a break, you know? With all our wives, it was very stressful. You're on the phone saying, 'I love you more than anything . . . but we gotta go now. See ya!'"

The tour cancellation, coupled with the fact that *Insomniac* hadn't sold quite as phenomenally as *Dookie*, fueled rampant speculation. Could this be the end of Green Day? But Billie Joe and the band were hardly ready to quit. Quite the contrary, in fact.

"I thought *Insomniac* was great," Armstrong insisted. "I think it's one of the most underrated records of the decade. People are saying it's our so called 'sophomore slump' album. But if anything it's our senior slump. It's our fourth record, but people think it's our second. So we need to step away from *Insomniac*, *Dookie*, *Kerplunk*, and *39/Smooth*. I think we need to redefine ourselves in a lot of ways. Take a position. Take a stance. Just come out with all the engines turned up."

> Billie Joe took time out of his schedule in 1996 to offer his engineering expertise to this 7-inch by Alameda psychobilly outfit the Tantrums. Guitarist Pete Rypins was a pal from Bay Area punk bands Crimpshrine and Tilt.

chapter 6

THE TIME OF THEIR LIVES

Green Day took a long, well-deserved break after the *Insomniac* tour fell apart. They changed management, opting for Pat Magnarella (then also managing Weezer and the Goo Goo Dolls) and Rob Cavallo's father, Bob, who had worked with Prince. It was a moment for the band to step back and regroup. Time out with family and friends recharged all their batteries, and Billie Joe came back with well over thirty new songs when the band reconvened to record their next album at L.A.'s top-notch Conway Studio with Rob Cavallo once again producing.

"Billie's constantly got three radio stations going on in his head, and they're all his own music," Dirnt said. "Billie's very introverted. He's one of those people you could be talking to for half an hour—I've seen him do this in interviews—and he'll suddenly say, 'I'm sorry, what were you saying, man?' That's because he's thinking music constantly. It's very natural for him. He's a more natural musician than anyone I've ever met in my life. And I've met a couple of musicians now."

> On the road, circa 1999.
© Rune Hellestad/Corbis

This time out, Armstrong's inner radios were tuned in to a wider spectrum of stations than on any previous Green Day album. The album that was to become *Nimrod* took the band four months to record, which was longer than the group had spent on any prior album. By rock 'n' roll standards, this wasn't much time at all, but by Gilman Street norms, it must have seemed sheer rock star extravagance to the band at times, a situation compounded by the fact that the band was staying at a posh superstar hotel, the Sunset Marquis in West Hollywood, while making the disc.

But with Armstrong's songwriting muse beckoning him in bold new directions, it took time to find just the right arrangement, setting, and instrumentation for each song. It was no longer a matter of just banging them down with guitar, bass, and drums—although there's plenty of that on *Nimrod* as well.

"I think we pushed ourselves as hard as we possibly could," Billie Joe noted in the record company's *Nimrod* press kit. "It was probably the most difficult record to make, the longest process we've ever undertaken, definitely. Each song has its own character and identity, so we wanted to be able to bring that out as much as possible."

With eighteen songs, *Nimrod* was Green Day's longest and most ambitious record yet— very nearly the double album Billie Joe had spoken of making after *Insomniac*. It also signaled the dawn of new, mature phase for Green Day. They no longer felt a need to adhere to punk or pop punk formulae, but by the same token they didn't stray so far from their original brief as to be unintelligible to longtime fans.

Most of *Nimrod* consists of great, slamming pop songs in the classic Green Day mold. But the deep tune stack allows for several intriguing points of departure. For instance, "King for a Day" is a song about a cross-dresser in the best rock tradition of Pink Floyd's "Arnold Layne" and the Kinks' "Lola," but set to a giddyup Wild West beat and embellished with a bumptious horn arrangement. The widescreen instrumental "Last Ride In" has a moody Ennio Morricone feel, complete with bongs, marimbas, strings, and brass. Dylan-esque harmonica crops up on "Walking Alone." Violinist Petra Haden, then with the Warners group That Dog, provides a brief, Middle Eastern–tinged solo intro to "Hitchin' a Ride," a great song about intemperance and falling off the wagon. And "Redundant" sports a quite George Harrison–like Leslie guitar effect over a stately descending chord progression.

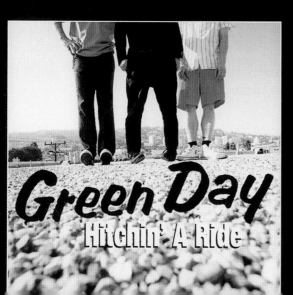

GREEN DAY

HITCHIN' A RIDE

THE COOL NEW SINGLE

TAKEN FROM THE

BRAND SPANKING

NEW ALBUM

NIMROD

Green Day
Hitchin' A Ride

HITCHIN' A RIDE

OUT NOW

NIMROD

OUT OCT 13TH

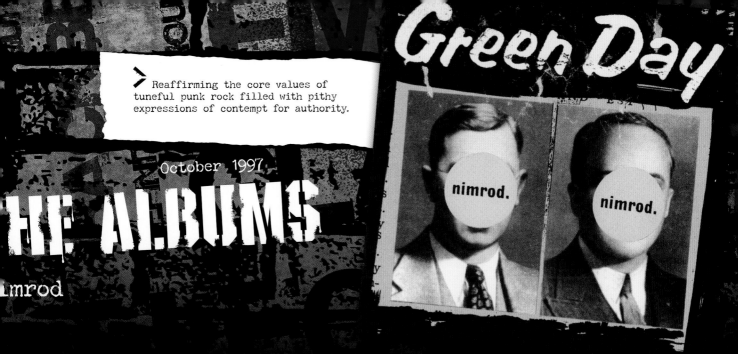

Green Day

Reaffirming the core values of
tuneful punk rock filled with pithy
expressions of contempt for authority.

October 1997

HE ALBUMS

imrod

re's a lot to digest on *Nimrod*. Green
's fifth album serves up a big eighteen
gs that venture all over the stylistic map.
ride takes a few mighty strange musical
ours along the way, but it also reaffirms
core Green Day values of loud, fast,
eful punk rock filled with clever, pithy
ressions of self-abnegation and outsider
tempt for authority. What's not to love?
Nimrod launches on a familiar pop punk
e with the briskly melodic "Nice Guys
sh Last," one of Billie Joe Armstrong's
y great "fuck you" numbers—although it
exactly clear whether the object of his
sion in this case is himself or some other
r fool. Either way, the song exhibits
strong's wonderful knack for hijacking
mmonplace expressions and turning them
heir ear. *Don't pat yourself on the back,*
ells the song's antagonist, *You might
ak your spine.* Classic Green Day all
way.

But we begin to get a hint that there's a
y different game afoot with *Nimrod*'s sec-
track, "Hitchin' a Ride." What's with that
dle Eastern violin (courtesy of Petra
en from the group That Dog) for an
o? Or that jazzy guitar chord at the
? These incongruent stylistic flourishes
cket a chugging, midtempo rock song
a descending "Hit the Road, Jack" chord
gression. This is a rhythmic feel that oc-
s frequently on *Nimrod*, balancing out the
re frenetic pop punk tunes. The slightly
re relaxed tempos seem to give Billie Joe's
bired melodicism a bit of breathing room
le also providing the listener with a little
re time to assimilate the tunesmith's ver-

bal barbs. *There's a drought at the fountain
of youth* runs one of the song's more memorable lines, *and I'm dehydrating.*

Whether the musical setting is blistering
hardcore or acoustic balladry, *Nimrod*'s over-
arching lyrical mood seems to be wistfully
retrospective. Five albums into his career,
Billie Joe is no longer the fresh-faced pop
punk wise guy of *39/Smooth* or *Dookie*. He
appears to be feeling the weight of the passing years. *Now it seems like I've forgotten
my purpose in life,* he sings on "Scattered."
Even the main visual conceit of the album
cover art—high school yearbook photos—un-
derscores the album's pervasive sentiment,
which might be described as antinostalgia,
far more bitter than sweet.

Billie Joe is looking back not so much in
anger (although there's certainly that) as in
regret and disillusionment. Even the album's
romantic songs are couched in terms of
missed opportunities and emotional dead
ends. And there's a brace of tunes ("Hitchin' a
Ride," "The Grouch," "All the Time," "Walking
Alone") that hint at alcoholic excess—always
a great source of dark emotions.

Midway through the album comes a fairly
startling departure for Green Day: a spaghet-
ti-western instrumental entitled "Last Ride
In." Tré Cool mans the bongos for this outing,
underpinning Billie Joe's big twang guitar.
Trombones growl ominously and strings (arranged by David Campbell) soar majestically.
It's no major masterpiece, but a refreshing
departure for Green Day.

As if to reassure us, though, they follow
up with four slamming tunes, the buzzy, pop
punk–paced "Jinx," "Haushinka," and "Reject,"

and the Ramones-go-Dylanesque "Walking
Alone." But then the home stretch is heavily mined with wild mood swings and crazy
stylistic juxtapositions. "Take Back" is pure
vindictive hardcore, complete with a Cookie
Monster chorus vocal that anticipates the
screamo movement by several years. From
here, we lurch right into "King for a Day,"
a celebration of cross-dressing—*GI Joe in
panty hose*—fitted out with a musical setting
that could serve as the soundtrack for a
rodeo clown turn, replete with elephant-fart
trombones and muted trumpets doing that
"little laughing dog" thing.

How could Green Day possibly follow
that? Why with the tearjerker acoustic ballad
"Good Riddance (Time of Your Life)," destined
to become one of the band's biggest hits
ever. But *Nimrod* comes to a halt on familiar
ground once again, with "Prosthetic Head,"
another of Billie Joe's great outsider kiss-offs
to the conformists and straights of the world.
Nimrod, after all, is an accepted slang term
for a jerk, a dickhead.

Are we all dickheads for following Green
Day down this bizarre musical rabbit hole?
Not in the least. After four albums of letter-
perfect pop punk, the lads certainly deserved
an opportunity to stretch out a bit. *Time
grabs you by the wrist,* as Billie Joe sings in
"Good Riddance." At this particular juncture in
Green Day's career, Armstrong doesn't quite
seem to know exactly where time is leading
him. But this uncertainty leads to some powerful musical moments, while also hinting at
greater achievements just down the road.

But by far the greatest departure for Green Day—and the album's biggest hit by a long chalk—was the acoustic ballad "Good Riddance (Time of Your Life)." Not specifically written for *Nimrod*, Armstrong began writing it, by some accounts, soon after his brief romance with the Gilman Street radical Amanda went awry.

"That song was written about an ex-girlfriend," Billie Joe confirmed, without naming names. "It was kind of a breakup song, but trying not to be angry about it. To me, when I hear it, it's obvious that I'm trying very hard to be levelheaded. And I'm a person who's not very levelheaded at all. It's one of those songs that just kind of wrote itself. And I ended up using it four years after the fact. I wrote it right around the time *Dookie* came out. It was sort of a song that I never thought anybody was gonna hear. It was just a personal thing."

◄ For *Nimrod*, Reprise trotted out one of their typical well-executed press kits, playing off both the yearbook angle of the LP art and the appearance of "Good Riddance (Time of Your Life)" on the hit NBC drama *ER*.

The solo acoustic arrangement with a string quartet enhancement was a radical departure, but it seemed the only possible way to present the song. Tré Cool joked that they considered giving "Good Riddance" a full band arrangement, "for about two seconds."

"It turned into a crappy rock ballad immediately," added Dirnt. "It's not that kind of song. It's a very intimate song—one person singing with their acoustic guitar. And the simplicity of it is heart-wrenching."

"Doing it with the whole band would have been impossible," Armstrong agreed. "It would have come out sounding like 'Living on a Prayer' or something. I pretty much said, 'There's only one way to do this song. And if we do it any other way, it's gonna be more cheesy than it already is.' It's still a good song, and I love it. I'm really proud of that song; it captured a moment in my life. There was a lot going on at that particular time for me. *Dookie* was coming out. All this stuff was happening. There were a lot of things I had to let go of and move on."

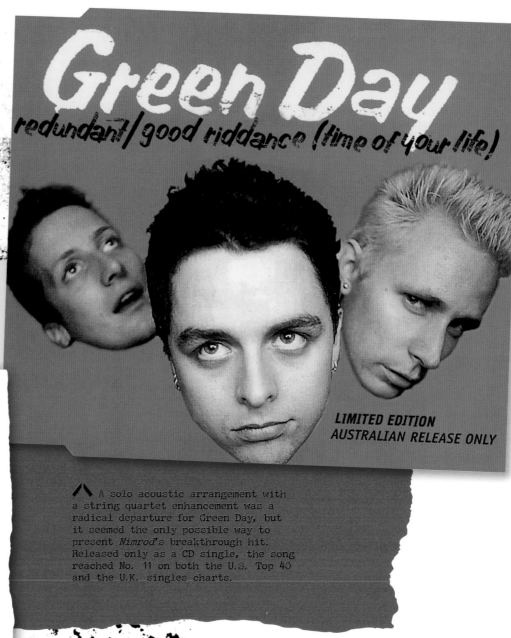

With *Nimrod*, Green Day would reel in at least one big one: "Good Riddance (Time of Your Life)." © Bureau L.A. Collection/Sygma/Corbis

A solo acoustic arrangement with a string quartet enhancement was a radical departure for Green Day, but it seemed the only possible way to present *Nimrod*'s breakthrough hit. Released only as a CD single, the song reached No. 11 on both the U.S. Top 40 and the U.K. singles charts.

KROQ Almost Acoustic X-mas, Universal Amphitheatre, Universal City, California, December 6, 1997. Jeff Kravitz/FilmMagic and Getty Images

Midtown Manhattan's Roseland Ballroom featured a little something for just about everyone in October and November 1997.

IF YOU HAVEN'T SEEN PRIMUS LATELY, YOU HAVEN'T SEEN PRIMUS!

PRIMUS *The Brown Tour* with **Buck-O-Nine** and **POWERMAN ☆5000☆** OCT 17

NEVER BEFORE SEEN PRE-HALLOWEEN SPECTACLE

GWAR **MISFITS** Mephiskapheles CRISIS
WARNING: THIS SHOW CONTAINS GRAPHIC MATERIAL. DEFINITELY NOT FOR THE SQUEAMISH! OCT 24

ECHO & THE BUNNYMEN
SPECIAL GUEST LONGPIGS SAT · OCT 25

TYPE O NEGATIVE
COAL CHAMBER
THE ELECTRIC HELLFIRE CLUB OCT 29

GREEN DAY ON SALE 10/16!
SUPERDRAG NOV 12

311 Sugar Ray WITH VERY SPECIAL GUEST
NOV 21 & 22

THE WALLFLOWERS
with special guest
BEN HARPER NOV 28 & 29 Roseland

239 West 52nd St., NYC (btwn 8th Ave. & B'way) TIX AVAILABLE AT THE ROSELAND BOX OFFICE & ALL ticketmaster LOCATIONS. CALL FOR TICKETS AT (212) 307-7171. FOR INFO CALL (212) 249-8870. www.livetonight.com

Cavallo and the band decided to leave in the false starts on guitar at the very beginning of the take. "They were rolling tape and they said, 'Just play it a bunch of times,'" Billie Joe recalled. "I played it and hit a wrong string and then started again. It was just a false start. Then we listened to it and I said, 'That's cool. Leave it in.'"

The string arrangement was provided by David Campbell, who worked on other *Nimrod* tracks as well. "David is Beck's dad," Billie Joe said. "When he first came in, he brought in like this twenty-piece orchestra. They were playing and it was like, 'Wow! Holy shit. This is insane.' I had to tell him, 'It sounds really amazing, but you're gonna have to get rid of about ten people.' We did and then it was, 'You know what? It sounds amazing, but you're going to have to get rid of about six more people.' So it ended up just being a little quartet following the melody and putting little pads on it. It was really classical, the way the violin player was playing at first. And I said, 'Can you make it more kinda squeaky sounding? Play with it. Can you put your thing on it and make it more sort of 'fiddle' sounding?' She said yeah. And she did."

◀ Poster advertising British Isles markets the band planned to visit in promotion of *Nimrod*.

▲ *Nimrod* world tour backstage passes.

The second single release from *Nimrod*, "Good Riddance," put Green Day in a whole different league when the song crossed over from rock radio to mainstream and even easy-listening formats. For most of Green Day's original punk audience, not to mention a significant number of the pop punk kids who'd glommed onto the band at the time of *Dookie*, it seemed that Green Day had gone seriously astray. The worst possible thing that a pop punk brat can do is grow up. Had Green Day gone "adult contemporary" or something?

But alienated hardliners seemed a small minority when set against the legions of new fans that "Good Riddance" drew to Green Day. Corny as it may seem, every tunesmith wants to capture some poignant emotion from his or her own life in a way that resonates in the hearts of people everywhere. "Good Riddance" became a staple at school graduations and other sentimental occasions. People seemed to ignore the kiss-off main title and focus on the more upbeat subtitle, which also forms the song's main lyrical hook line.

On the strength of "Good Riddance" and its crossover success, Green Day were able to take the luxury of a long hiatus once touring for *Nimrod* wound down. It was a time for all three members of Green Day to get their houses and family lives in order.

"My marriage was pretty rocky," Billie Joe later confessed. "I really needed to concentrate on that. I needed to stay home for a while. I needed to step away from music for a while—to be hungry again."

The band members' families grew and changed during this period. A daughter, Estelle Desiree, was born to Mike Dirnt and his wife Anastasia in April 1997. Billie Joe and Adrienne's second son, Jakob Danger Armstrong, came along in September 1998. Meanwhile, Tré Cool's marriage to Lisa Lyons fell apart and he married his second wife, Claudia. Their son Frankito was born in 2001. "If we hadn't taken time off, I never would have got to meet my wife," Cool said.

It was a fertile period creatively as well, albeit outside the Green Day context. Billie Joe and Adrienne launched the punk indie label Adeline Records in 1997, naming the venture for a street in the Berkeley/Oakland area. The label released a slew of discs, including several by Billie Joe's longtime side band Pinhead Gunpowder, while Armstrong produced releases by several bands on the label, including the Dillinger Four, One Man Army, Dead and Gone, and the Criminals. Adeline also released a disc by Dirnt's side band, the Frustrators, which the bassist described as sounding "like a cross between Blondie and the Rezillos."

∨ Nimrod tour T-shirts, circa 1997. Both WycoVintage.com

Neil Young's Bridge School benefit, Shoreline Amphitheatre, Mountain View, California, October 30, 1999. Jay Blakesberg/ blakesberg.com

The Frustrators even played a gig at Gilman Street in this period. "It was a fucking great show," Dirnt enthused. "Two hundred and fifty people in there. For me, it was really a wonderful piece of closure. And you know what? I didn't get one iota of shit all night long. You know why? 'Cause the people where we come from know we're not full of shit. They know that we support the scene by backing ourselves off from it. We love where we come from. We love punk rock. I don't think there's anything that we've done that's not positive in the long run."

So while Green Day scaled ever greater heights of mainstream success, the band's members were able to retain a modicum of underground punk cred through side projects. But the period had a lot of ups and downs for Dirnt. On the positive side, the chest pains that he had been suffering turned out to be relatively minor disorder. On the other hand, his marriage to Anastasia collapsed. The divorce settlement enabled Mike and his ex-wife to share custody of their child.

"I moved five times in the past three years," he said in 2000. "I split with my ex-wife. It was an amicable split, but it was a split nonetheless. I moved. I lived in a crappy apartment for a year. Then I sold my house. Then I lived in another tiny house. Then I moved out to Oakland to live with my girlfriend, Sarah. So it's real nice."

chapter 7

FAT ELVIS PERIOD

While Green Day didn't record or tour during the long hiatus following *Nimrod*'s release, they continued to see one another regularly in their rehearsal space. Despite their multiplatinum status, band practice remained an almost daily institution. "We only took a month and a half off from each other [after *Nimrod*]," Dirnt said. "Then we started practicing five days a week. Band practice isn't an event for us. It's what we do. We enjoy it, but we take it very seriously. We always have. Even when me and Billie were like ten. After school we'd be like, 'Dude, let's jam.' And it was definitely gonna happen."

During the lengthy layoff period, songs for the next Green Day album began to emerge in a more relaxed organic way than they had before. "For *Nimrod*, I was writing songs constantly," Armstrong said, "just powering through them. But for this album, I would wait for the moment."

"Billie took a trip with his family to see his wife's family in Minnesota," Dirnt added. "He came back and said, 'I've got five or six new ideas. Let's jam on them.' Some things he put down on a four-track. Whereas on our last record, we wrote a shitload of songs and said, 'Later we'll see which ones are standing out.' But this time we just let the songs happen."

Somewhere in Orange County,
California, June 2000. Kevin
Estrada/KevinEstrada.com

The result of this process was *Warning*, Green Day's sixth album, a disc that arguably inaugurates the "classic rock" phase of Green Day's career. While still rooted firmly in punk, *Warning* is replete with overt echoes of the Kinks, Beatles, Who, and Stones—not just a facile or slavish imitation of those sounds from rock's bygone golden age, but a clear-sighted and deft assimilation of the songwriting sensibility that made classic rock classic in the first place. Billie Joe had always been a bit cagey about his old-school influences. But now he openly admitted he was listening to a lot of Bob Dylan during the making of *Warning*. He was finding the courage to step into the songwriting arena of the giants.

"It's more of a folk record," said Dirnt of *Warning*. "But it's definitely Green Day and it definitely rocks. It's not like we came out and wrote a bunch of jangly crap. They're good songs. I think they're the best ones Billie's ever written. Some of the lyrics really strike a nerve in me."

∨ Performing under the watchful eye of Gene on the Vans Warped Tour, Fairplex, Pomona, California, June 29, 2000. Kelly Swift/Retna Ltd.

❯ Warped Tour Poster, Pier 30/32, San Francisco, July 1, 2000.

Green Day performed in front of San Francisco's Civic Center on November 5, 2000, as part of the Million Band March. The "anti-gentrification" event was designed to bring attention to an increasing lack of affordable practice spaces and studios for musicians and artists as a result of the dot-com boom. Photo: Scott Harrison/Archive/Getty Images

"There's an element of hope in this record," added Tré Cool, a man not usually given to sentimental or philosophical pronouncements.

Along with the more relaxed pace of songwriting, and the mature, comfortably domestic mood of the long post-*Nimrod* layoff, a few other factors contribute to *Warning*'s marked difference from previous (and indeed subsequent) Green Day albums. For one, it was recorded with minimal involvement from Rob Cavallo, who hitherto had played a far more hands-on role.

"Rob is sort of an executive producer on this one," Armstrong explained. "Or sort of a production consultant. We did this whole thing ourselves. Just me, Mike, Tré, and Ken [Allardyce], our engineer. Rob came up on a couple of different occasions, just if we asked any questions. 'Cause you get a little crazy in the studio—too much microscoping. So you need an outside perspective. Someone you trust."

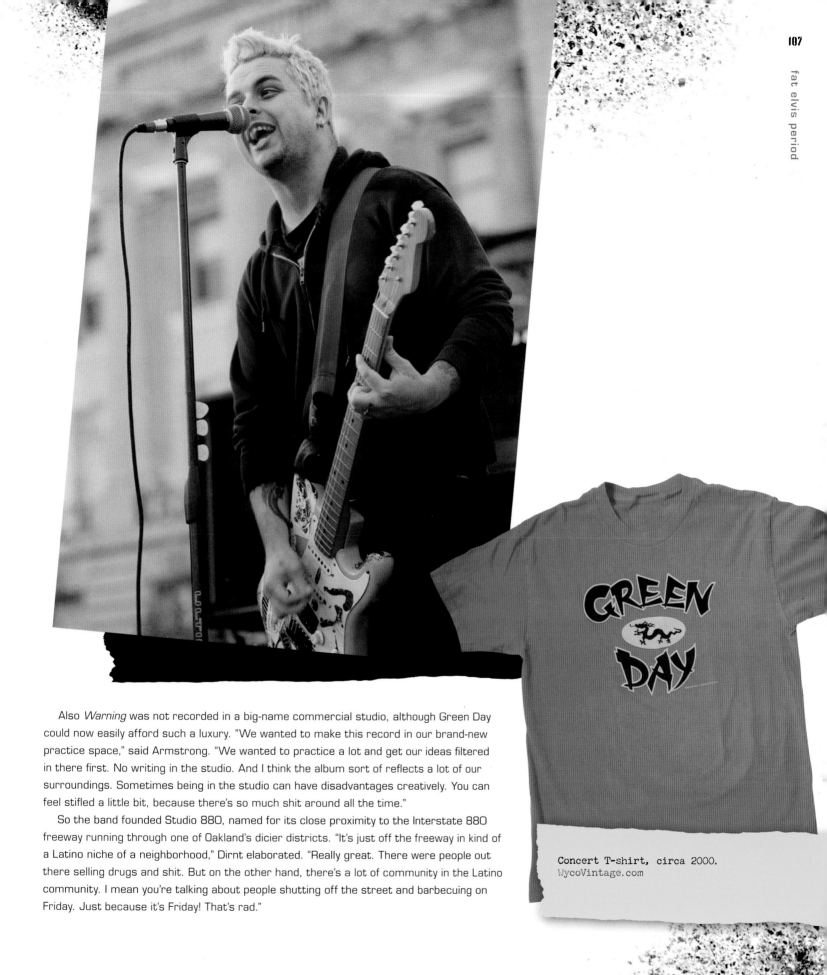

Concert T-shirt, circa 2000.
WycoVintage.com

Also *Warning* was not recorded in a big-name commercial studio, although Green Day could now easily afford such a luxury. "We wanted to make this record in our brand-new practice space," said Armstrong. "We wanted to practice a lot and get our ideas filtered in there first. No writing in the studio. And I think the album sort of reflects a lot of our surroundings. Sometimes being in the studio can have disadvantages creatively. You can feel stifled a little bit, because there's so much shit around all the time."

So the band founded Studio 880, named for its close proximity to the Interstate 880 freeway running through one of Oakland's dicier districts. "It's just off the freeway in kind of a Latino niche of a neighborhood," Dirnt elaborated. "Really great. There were people out there selling drugs and shit. But on the other hand, there's a lot of community in the Latino community. I mean you're talking about people shutting off the street and barbecuing on Friday. Just because it's Friday! That's rad."

> Love it or hate it, a deliberate and decisive move away from a winning pop punk formula.

October 2000

THE ALBUMS

Warning

Green Day's transitional album *Warning* draws a bold line in the sand. People tend either to love it or hate it. The disc certainly isn't the familiar old Green Day of the band's first five albums. *Warning* seems a deliberate and decisive move away from the winning pop punk formula that made the band one of the most successful rock acts of the '90s. Gone are the big, buzzy guitars, thudding drums, and breakneck tempos. Instead, the approach focuses on acoustic guitars and cleaner-sounding electrics. There is much more rhythmic variety as well.

And there are plenty of reasons to love *Warning*. In a sense, it's Green Day's *Rubber Soul*. On that 1965 album, the Beatles made their big break away from the lovable mop-pop sounds of Beatlemania, embracing acoustic guitars, a wider range of instrumentation, and exotic tonalities from far-off corners of the world. Green Day do much the same on *Warning*, and the net result is quite similar in both cases. The listener is drawn more intimately into the songcraft. This, in turn, allows a more nuanced, mature songwriting voice to emerge.

Maturity is a key term here. For the first time, Billie Joe Armstrong isn't singing

exclusively about his own personal issues, hang-ups, and insecurities. He's learned to look outward and to write about what he sees in other people and the world at large. In this sense, he becomes a little more like one of his key songwriting mentors, Ray Davies—a social satirist, observer, and narrator. Being American rather than English, however, Armstrong comes up with something uniquely his own and something distinctly American on *Warning*—a wistful window-on-main-street mood that invites comparison to American fiction writers like Sherwood Anderson and John Cheever.

As Billie Joe looks out on main street, he doesn't particularly like what he sees. More than anything else, *Warning* is an indictment of America's rampantly materialistic consumer society of the late 1990s. It chronicles and satirizes the orgy of crass acquisitiveness that led to the credit card crunch and "21st Century Breakdown" that Billy Joe would write about a few years down the road.

As much as *Warning*'s "Fashion Victim" is an update of Davies' "Dedicated Follower of Fashion," Armstrong's song cuts a little deeper by getting at the price of fashion fetishism. Armstrong's fashion victims are

cloaked with style . . . as the credit card explodes. They've *auctioned off [their] life for the most expensive price*. The album's closing track, "Macy's Day Parade," sounds a similar and eerily prophetic note: *The night of the living dead is on its way, with a credit report for duty call*.

Warning's title track takes on another dark side of consumerism: the '90s proliferation of cautionary labels and stickers affixed to products of all sorts, as manufacturers sought to indemnify themselves from lawsuits by consumers and activists. The result, referenced in the album cover art, is a grotesque cartoon language of strangling babies and stickmen zapped by lightning or tumbling off ladders. "Warning" cooks along to a driving acoustic guitar riff as Billie Joe warns us against the warnings and the warners. The instrumentation may be slightly different, but the message is the same punk rock cry for freedom that's always been at the heart of Green Day's songcraft.

From the S&M freak in "Blood, Sex and Booze" to the desperate misfits who populate "Misery," *Warning*'s colorful cast of characters all seem to be seeking to fill an inner void with something suspiciously superficial

"Warning" b/w "Scumbag" and "Outsider," Adeline, 2000

"Waiting" b/w "Maria," Adeline, 2001.

Musically, "Misery" is one of *Warning*'s tours de force—a Felliniesqe romp that could have been penned by soundtrack composer Nino Rota, richly shaded with Mediterranean mandolins, carnivalesque accordions, and deftly orchestrated strings. In all of this, "Misery" anticipates the "gypsy punk" sounds of groups like Gogol Bordello by quite a few years.

While Billy Joe is very much an observer on *Warning*, he never puts himself above the crowd. As a result, when he does write from a more personal perspective—in "Church on Sunday" and "Castaway," for instance—the result becomes more poignant. His issues are our issues in many ways, whether it's struggling to keep a relationship vital or dealing with feelings of alienation.

So if consumerism isn't the way to fill those inner voids, what is? As always, Billie Joe advocates the fierce sense of nonconformist individualism so central to punk rock. *When you lost all hope and . . . /Nothing's left to cling to/You got to/Hold on to yourself*, he sings in the Beatlesesque "Hold On." Another of *Warning*'s standout tracks, "Minority," strikes a proudly antiauthoritarian tone. With a sly poke at political correctness, Armstrong

convenes an outsider army of all races, creeds, and colors. The tune itself might be a rebel melody appropriated from the Irish independence struggle. The folk-picked intro and outro remind us that, long before punk rock or even the electric guitar, the acoustic guitar was a splendid weapon of resistance.

While freeing up Armstrong's songwriting and voice, *Warning*'s acoustic approach also seems to liberate Tré Cool, offering an opportunity to show his versatility and resourcefulness as a drummer. And as always, Mike Dirnt is right there when you need him, with the perfect bass line and vocal harmony for each and every song. The acoustic settings further bring his superb backing vocals a little more to the fore as well.

So when you strip away the familiar pop punk trappings of prior Green Day albums, you're still left with a great band playing great songs. And that's what Green Day are really all about.

7 Backstage pass, 2001.

➤ *Warning* mini poster, Japanese tour, March 2001.

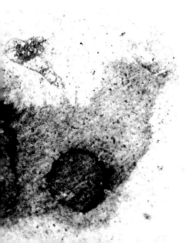

But working in a studio where "the freeway runs right over it," in Armstrong's words, presented sonic challenges as well. "Every time a truck goes by, you can feel it on the [mixing] board," Billie Joe marveled. "I shit you not. You can hear it in the frequencies the microphones pick up. We said, 'This is a great place. It's ten minutes from where we live. We can be at home and still do our thing there and also be in the studio and not be distracted in any way. So we asked the owner, 'Would you be willing to put the money into remodeling here and there?' He said yeah."

The studio was blessed with a state-of-the-art SSL G+ Series mixing console, but was in need of some acoustic treatment. "We brought a guy in and had him rebuild the room pretty much," said Dirnt. "We told the owner of the studio, 'Look, we'll record here, but we need you to put in new hardwood floors and we want to bring in a guy to do some sound modification. Now I think it's one of the best rooms in the Bay Area. When we found it, it was an okay room with a great board. Now it's a great room with a great board . . . and an okay lounge."

Sporting Chucks, somewhere in
the U.K., August 2001.

In time, Studio 880 would become Green Day's general HQ, a large industrial building down at the end of a funky street, complete with offices, equipment storage, and everything else that goes with running a world-class rock band. But all that was still a little way down the road. For *Warning*, the band at least—and for the very first time—had a studio they could call their own.

"The thing is it wasn't plagued with anyone else's stink who was in there before," Armstrong noted. "Especially in the Bay Area, every studio we checked out, it was like, 'Oh this is Santana's favorite room.' We said, 'Oh great. Um, see ya later.' I think every studio said that. One studio we went to, the woman was obviously doing the same spiel for the past twenty years: 'Oh yeah, we had everyone from Sammy Hagar, Huey Lewis and the News, to Journey, Santana. . . .' Every name she was saying, we were like, 'Eww . . . Ouch . . . See ya.'"

▼ Mike takes off at the Gig on the Green, Glasgow, August 26, 2001. The show also featured Eminem, Iggy Pop, Marilyn Manson, Papa Roach, and Travis. *Graham Knowles/Redferns/Getty Images*

▲ Bill Graham Civic Auditorium, San Francisco, August 5, 2001. John Shearer/WireImage/Getty Images

Safely ensconced in their barrio hideaway, Green Day came up with some of the most interesting songs in their entire canon. *Warning*'s title track deftly and humorously hones in on a deep-seated sense of paranoia inherent in contemporary American culture, and that just a year later would go ballistic in the post 9/11 era. In that regard, it is one of Armstrong's most prescient songs.

"I just wrote it one day," Armstrong said. "Adrienne's brother made me the strongest pot of coffee I'd ever had in my life. You know how it is when you drink so much coffee you gotta lay down for a second? Anyway, I always had this idea of writing a song from the sayings off people's bumper stickers. Put them all together. A song called 'Bumper Stickers'—as a joke, you know? And there are a lot of warning labels out there. I tried to put my own twist on them. I wanted to say something in the same way as 'crucify me,' in that song by the Beatles ['The Ballad of John and Yoko']."

A compressed litany of familiar cautionary phrases from prescription drug labels, owners' manuals, emergency broadcasts, and other sources, each verse in "Warning" ends with the tag line, *Warning: live without warning*. And, lest anyone miss the point, the second verse advises, *Question everything, or shut up and be a victim of authority*.

"We live in a world where there are caution signs everywhere," Billie Joe said. "You have sort of subliminal limitations. I guess it's the old rule that laws and rules are meant to be broken—not just in music, but in everything. Those limitations can be so suffocating. And it does sort of affect your freedom as a citizen of the United States. Here's this country that flies on its freedom and its propaganda for freedom all the time. But I've been to other countries where there's more sense of freedom than there is at home, as far as television, bars, nightlife, and things like that."

The *Warning* album marked a key turning point in Armstrong's songwriting. He trained his eye less on his own personal issues and more on what was happening in the world around him. And he didn't necessarily like what he saw. More antiauthoritarian social commentary emerges on the anthemic "Minority," one of *Warning*'s most popular tracks. The song's defiant mood foreshadows some of *American Idiot*'s most jubilantly militant tracks. In true punk rock spirit, Armstrong casts his lot in with society's outcasts, outsiders and marginalized groups: *I don't need your authority/Down with the moral majority/'Cause I want to be the minority.*

"It's kind of about being an individual," said Armstrong of the song. "Stepping away from a crowd or stepping out of line. Having your own views and standing up for yourself. And not being thrown into a classist society. Being a patriot for yourself—your own pride in yourself, not for any sort of ethnic background. Just being an individual. Your own minority. Your own opinions and views."

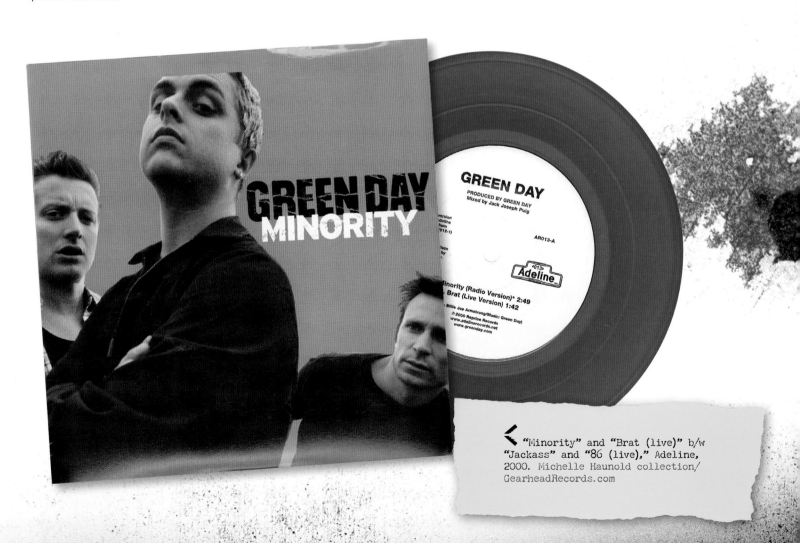

◄ "Minority" and "Brat (live)" b/w "Jackass" and "86 (live)," Adeline, 2000. Michelle Haunold collection/ GearheadRecords.com

Armstrong's social observations turned from a defiant mood to a wistful one on the acoustic-driven "Macy's Day Parade." "A lot of that is my commentary on commercialism," he said. "A lot of people find a false sense of security, a false sense of freedom, in consumerism—buying stuff. I just feel that I go through life wanting something, but I don't know what it is. But I guess it's hope in general. Anything that's hopeful. Nothing specific. And nothing material."

The freedom of being on their own in Studio 880 gave rise to some interesting audio verité moments, such as when the band summoned two professional ladies to the studio to spice up the intro to "Blood, Sex and Booze."

"That's a real dominatrix on there you know," Billie Joe revealed. "Tré called up this dominatrix. I think it was probably someone he knew. And these two women came in and beat the shit out of our second engineer. We put up mics and recorded it. We just happened to get a little [spoken] tidbit at the beginning and a couple of whip cracks, and we put that in the song. We said, 'Hey, that's really cool!' It was just one of those things. Studio magic!"

The song itself, Armstrong explained, "is about how people use pain as a sort of healing process. A lot of it is speaking metaphorically. But some of it is kind of real."

Asked if he was concerned that the song would make listeners wonder if he was personally into S&M, Armstrong shrugged dismissively. "I don't know. . . . A lot of people think I masturbate five times a day, because of the words to 'Longview,' you know?"

As in the past, the band finished up the album at Ocean Way, where they proceeded to stake out more new musical territory, particularly on "Misery." The song begins with a vintage '60s Farfisa organ prelude played by Dirnt, which gives way to a loping Old World, minor-key feel that wouldn't be out of place in a Brecht/Weill cabaret opera.

"We were thinking we could do anything we want with that song," Armstrong explained, "because there was so much open space between what the three of us were playing. So we added a mandolin and then brought in an Italian funeral band to do some overdubs. And then someone said it would be cool to make it go in a different direction and add a mariachi band. It was pretty interesting to watch all the musicians come in, all these weird session people. This Italian funeral band comes in and plays their part. Then this mariachi band comes in and they play. And some string session people come in and finish their part."

"It was all done under the masterful mind of David Campbell," Dirnt added.

Billie Joe himself played the mandolin part, despite the fact that he'd never played the instrument before. "I just sort of winged it, you know?" he said. "Someone had to play it."

The song is also Brechtian in its lowlife plot line, setting, and cast of characters, while the use of characterization and narrative make "Misery" a key *American Idiot* precursor. "The lyrics pretty much just tell a story," Billie Joe said, "I think Virginia is the character who ends up somewhere good . . . I think."

The character name Mr. Whirly was lifted from a Replacements song, Armstrong disclosed. "The Replacements did a song called 'Mr. Whirly,' where they used the same vocal hook as 'Oh! Darling' by the Beatles, but they did it like a drunk version, singing 'Mr. Whirly.' So if they could rip off the Beatles, I figured I could rip off the Replacements. Hopefully, someone will take it and put it in a song ten years later and rip me off too."

▲ Billie Joe's baby blue Fernandez "on its last legs," circa 2000. It was around this time that he developed his now-famous affinity for Les Paul Juniors.

The 46-date Pop Disaster Tour featured Green Day co-headlining with Blink 182. Shoreline Amphitheatre, Mountain View, California, April 27, 2002. Touring guitarist Jason White is at left. © Tim Mosenfelder/Corbis

But not all the sonic innovation on *Warning* is in the acoustic instrumental realm. The album also found Billie Joe forsaking his beloved Fernandez Strat in favor of Gibson Les Paul Junior electric guitars. Originally developed as a more affordable, less ornate alternative to the Gibson Les Paul, the Junior, with its P-90 pickups, has an edgier sound than the bass-heavy humbucking pickups used on most Les Paul models. The Les Paul Junior also has a great punk rock pedigree, having been the choice of innovators like Johnny Thunders of the New York Dolls and Heartbreakers and Steve Diggle of the Buzzcocks. In time, Armstrong would become increasingly obsessive over Les Paul Juniors, amassing a sizable horde of highly collectible vintage models and playing them extensively on later works, such as *American Idiot* and *21st Century Breakdown*. In this sense, too, *Warning* serves as a dividing line between Green Day's earlier sound and their more mature phase.

"My baby blue Stratocaster was on its last legs," Billie said, "And I was developing too many superstitions about it. And there's just something about a P-90 through a Fender Bassman amp. This is a total P-90 record. There's so much you can do with the volume control. You just go down a notch and it's a completely different tone. But I love all guitars. I think each one has its purpose."

For all *Warning*'s social commentary, it also contains several of Armstrong's most personal songs. "Church on Sunday" deals with issues in Billie Joe's and Adrienne's marriage in fairly straightforward terms. "It's about just trying to keep my relationship with my wife, just still renewing it all the time," he explained. "And coming up with compromises for each other—for all my quirks. . . . I think all of us have grown up a little bit, as individuals. And it's kind of made us a stronger unit, ironically."

But the song that is perhaps *Warning*'s keynote track is "Hold On," with its themes of keeping hope alive and maintaining a belief in yourself even when things seem to be at their most grim. "That song was about a friend of mine, who had three friends of his die within one year," Billie Joe revealed. "It's hard to watch your friends go through pain like that. You can't say anything to them to actually make them feel better. Because it just takes time to heal from something so harsh that happens in your life. The only thing you can do is just get a grip on yourself somehow."

Acceptance of death had been an issue for Armstrong ever since he was ten years old and his father died. "Hold On" meant enough to him that he went back to rerecord the harmonica part so that it would be less of a direct rip on the Beatles' "I Should Have Known Better." "It was just too much," he said. "The song is a pretty meaningful one. I didn't want it to get overshadowed because of some stupid harmonica part."

All in all, *Warning* marks a significant move away from the self-loathing brattiness of earlier Green Day songs. Maturing into adult life as family men, all the members of Green Day seemed to be striving toward a more positive outlook, without losing the essential rebellious tendencies of the punk rock legacy.

"I just said, 'Enough's enough. I want to live my life,'" Billy Joe confided to me at the time. "I do everything like it's my last day on Earth. And I want my music to represent me. I'm now at an age where I want to say something that my son Joey is gonna look at and say, 'That's my dad and I'm very proud. This is so cool, something that he sang. It's powerful and strong and it means something.' So that's the way I look at it. I don't want to just leave a mess. I want to leave good feelings out of what I get out of my life before I die. And I don't plan on dying any time soon. . . . There's always a sense of rebellion that is not decadent and is not the neon signs you see on Sunset Boulevard. It's a personal belief. I need to grow. It's either that or I'm gonna be digging a deeper hole. I want growth, and I want that to reflect in my music."

The problem was that Green Day's core fan base didn't particularly want to grow up. Despite the popularity of the anthemic "Minority," *Warning* proved to be less successful than *Nimrod*. Reluctant to let go of its perception of Green Day as snotty, pop punk cutups, a substantial portion of the record-buying public simply wasn't ready for a mature, reflective Green Day. That wasn't why they'd gotten onboard back in '94. And in the time since then, a boatload of highly successful pop punk acts had sprung up to satisfy this audience's craving for fast, loud, tuneful, sardonically dumb songcraft and lovable goofball personae. At the upper end of the spectrum there were Blink 182 and the Offspring, and a few levels down, everyone from MxPx to Sum 41. Nasal, and often pathetic, imitations of Billie Joe's distinctive vocal delivery were thick on the ground.

Indeed, when Green Day joined the 2000 Warped Tour, they often found themselves playing second fiddle to Blink 182. But while all these latter-day pop punk acts owed a major stylistic debt to Green Day, Armstrong was reluctant to claim credit even where credit may have been due. "I've had so many good things happen with my band," he said, "I don't feel like anybody owes me anything. When I hear Blink 182, I don't think they sound like Green Day. I think they sound like NOFX. There are so many subfactions of punk rock right now—at least three different styles of playing pop punk music. I think it would be unfair to them and us to really compare us. That would be like saying that all hip-hop or all country music sounds the same."

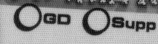

Armstrong tried to make the best of the Warped Tour, reporting that the biggest party animals were "probably the Long Beach Dub Allstars and Suicide Machines. They've been having a beer bong competition every day. They sort of split it up into different categories and give the bands these beer bongs. But it's not like a fraternity party. Just sort of for fun."

Still, at a time when Armstrong and his band were breaking new stylistic ground, they found themselves mostly playing hits from their back catalog on the Warped Tour, honoring requests hollered by the crowd. "I'm really eager to get out there on our own tour and be able to start playing these new songs," Billie Joe admitted. "Just do our own thing. It becomes hard to watch some of the same bands every single day."

When it finally came time to tour behind *Warning*, Armstrong was determined not to make the same mistakes that Green Day had made on previous tours, overworking and overextending themselves. "We're definitely going to pace ourselves and not tour for fourteen months straight this time," he said.

But when touring for *Warning* did wind down, Dirnt had to undergo surgery for carpal tunnel syndrome, a disorder that afflicts many guitarists, bassists, and other instrumentalists.

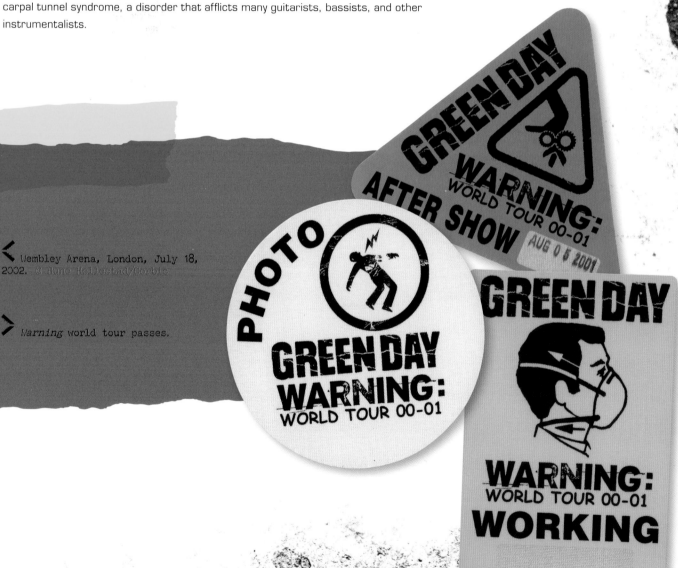

◄ Wembley Arena, London, July 18, 2002. © Ryan Hellestad/Corbis

► *Warning* world tour passes.

Dirnt's recovery, combined with a sense of inertia engendered by disappointing sales of *Warning*, put Green Day in the doldrums for the first few years of twenty-first century. The release of the compilation album *International Superhits!* and B-side anthology *Shenanigans* furthered the impression of a band treading water creatively. During this period, Billie Joe Armstrong appeared bloated and spent, his hair somewhat ill-advisedly dyed blond and his cheeks chubby. He looked his age, or older, and was certainly no longer the teenage punk heartthrob who'd excited frenzy in young girls and jealous admiration in young boys a decade or so earlier. Never one to miss a great opportunity for self-derision, Armstrong would later refer to this period as "my fat Elvis period," echoing a comment John Lennon had made about his mid-'60s career. In 1980, Lennon had compared his *Help!* period, when he'd put on weight and become a bit insecure, to Elvis Presley in his post–rock 'n' roll, jumpsuit period. With his characteristic flair for referencing rock history, Billie Joe was putting himself, albeit ironically, in the pantheon of rock icons who had gone a bit flabby and lost the plot. Who else but Armstrong would place himself in the company of giants only to put himself down?

The greatest irony, however, was that Green Day were on the cusp of a new career high, much as the Beatles had been in 1966—a new phase that would eclipse all Green Day had done before while also consolidating the punk rock glory of their earlier work. They were on the brink of a major artistic breakthrough, something that would evoke, while simultaneously transcending, the broad sweep of rock history up to that point. But as the new century dawned, few could have guessed any of this. Perhaps, least of all, Green Day themselves.

◥ Dirnt's recovery from carpal tunnel syndrome, combined with the disappointing sales of *Warning*, put Green Day in the doldrums for the first few years of twenty-first century. The release of the compilation album *International Superhits!* and B-side anthology *Shenanigans* furthered the impression of a band treading water.

◤ After playing London's Wembley Arena in July 2002, Green Day headlined the Distortion festival in the U.K., with punk godfather Iggy Pop in support.

PUNK ROCK GOES TO THE OPERA

The year 2003 did not dawn auspiciously for Green Day. In the early morning hours of January 5, Billie Joe Armstrong was arrested on a DUI charge in Oakland after being caught exceeding the legal speed limit in his BMW. He was briefly jailed, then released on bail and sentenced to community service. During this same period, Tré Cool was embroiled in divorce proceedings with Claudia. Wife Number Two, Frankito's mom, was about to become history.

But perhaps the unkindest cut came later in the year. The band had been laboring to record a new album, one that would hopefully propel Green Day out of their commercial and creative post-*Warning* doldrums. Armstrong, Dirnt, and Cool had just about finished this new record, which was to have been titled *Cigarettes and Valentines*, when the master tapes suddenly and mysteriously went missing.

"We had something like twenty songs, and one day they just disappeared," Billie Joe recounted. "We thought about rerecording them, but we couldn't honestly look at ourselves and say, 'That was the best thing we've ever done.' So we decided to move on and do something completely new."

Sometimes misfortunes can be blessings in disguise. The loss of the *Cigarettes and Valentines* master tapes set in motion a chain of events that would lead to the creation of what is perhaps Green Day's greatest work ever, *American Idiot*. But the journey to that career-redefining masterpiece was to take a somewhat circuitous route. After the *C&V* masters went AWOL, *Money Money 20/20*, a new album ostensibly by a masked, German, post–New Wave synth band called the Network, was widely speculated to be the work of Green Day—an absurdist, pseudonymous parody in Devo/Kraftwerk drag. The members of Green Day have always vehemently denied that they are indeed the Network, or even a part thereof. Yet the lead vocals and songwriting style of songs on *Money Money 20/20* contain some fairly flagrant Armstrongisms. And the album was released on Billie and Adrienne's label Adeline Records. The mysterious, masked Network once opened for Green Day in 2004, and the Foxboro Hot Tubs, Green Day's 2008 alter ego garage band, was known to cover Network songs. But where Green Day freely admitted that they were indeed Foxboro Hot Tubs, they've never claimed to be the Network.

Green Day, circa *American Idiot*.
Passionate political tirades never lapsing
into mere dogma. © Kim Kulish/CORBIS

> Kicking off the *American Idiot*
tour, Henry Fonda Theater, Hollywood,
California, September 16, 2004. John
Shearer/WireImage/Getty Images

Whatever Green Day's level of involvement, the Network record seemed to have been just the palette cleanser the band needed to distance themselves from *Cigarettes and Valentines* and come up with something better. "We were still in the vein of doing the sound of *Warning* on the earlier record," Billie Joe explained. "But for this new one, we were like, 'Let's just go balls out. Let's plug in the Les Pauls and Marshall amps and let it rip.' That's Green Day for me."

In songwriting terms, Billie Joe hit a home run right out of the box. The angry and infectious tune "American Idiot" would become the title track and keynote song for the album soon to emerge. A scathing invective set to slashing guitars, "American Idiot" draws a direct bead on the corporate media–orchestrated wave of mass paranoia and intolerance that followed in the wake of the U.S. Supreme Court nomination of George W. Bush as the forty-third president of the United States in 2000.

The second member of the Bush dynasty to hold the nation's highest office and the only U.S. president ever to rule by judicial fiat rather than popular election, Bush and right-wing media partners like Rupert Murdoch's News Corporation exploited the tragic terrorist attacks of September 11, 2001, to advance their own pro-corporate, anti–civil liberties agenda denouncing criticism, debate, and contrarian views as "unpatriotic." This carefully orchestrated reactionary wave ultimately led to Bush's ill-advised declaration of war on Iraq in 2003, pursuing his father's, former President George H. W. Bush, vendetta against Iraqi strongman Saddam Hussein and plunging the United States into a sustained economic depression that would grip the country and its global allies for many years to come.

Billie Joe gets into character, Irving Plaza, New York City, September 21, 2004. KMazur/ WireImage/Getty Images

THE NETWORK
MONEY MONEY 2020

PARENTAL
ADVISORY
EXPLICIT CONTENT

Chilling north of the border.
Toronto, September 23, 2004. The band
played that city's Phoenix Theatre
the following evening. AP Photo/CP/
Adrian Wyld

Green Day and friends as an
absurdist parody in Kraftwerk
post-New Wave drag.

In one brave and brilliant punk rock song, Billie Joe went after the Bush regime and all it had wrought, like the biblical David aiming his slingshot at the giant Goliath. Riding the revolutionary rhythm of electric guitars, bass, and drums, Armstrong indicts "subliminal mind fuck America," proudly declaring his determination not to become the titular American idiot.

"'American Idiot' just came out of watching the disturbing coverage on CNN, Fox, and MSNBC when the Iraq war first started," he said. "It was sort of news, but they had all these Geraldo Rivera–like journalists who were with the tanks and the soldiers, with the cameras, getting the play-by-play. It was like commentary on a football game or something. I felt like they'd finally crossed that line between journalism and reality TV. Everybody was glued to the TV, watching this thing go down. So we're living in the ultimate time of reality television. Something as horrific as 9/11—people were glued to the television watching this tragedy. I was too. But at the same time, there's still commercials in between, which is really confusing. They're strategically placed too, which is even more confusing. So you feel like you're losing your sense of your own individuality."

A gloriously populist, three-chord broadside—a melodic and spiritual successor to Clash rabble-rousers like "White Riot" and "London's Burning"— "American Idiot" proved a tough act to follow in songwriting terms. Once you've penned an unforgettable song that passionately sums up the zeitgeist of your given era, what do you do next? Fortunately, Mike Dirnt found the way forward: comic relief.

Left to his own devices at Studio 880 on a day when Billie Joe was off fulfilling his community-service requirement and Cool was meeting with divorce lawyers, Dirnt came up with a lightweight snippet of a tune called "Nobody Likes You," which would become part of "Homecoming," an extended suite and American Idiot's penultimate track.

"We were all so worried about how we were going to come up with songs to match ['American Idiot']," Armstrong related. "So Mike was in the studio by himself one day and he did a thirty-second song, and it had a kind of vaudeville sound to it. It was kind of funny. So I said, 'Well let me do something like that too. I wanna do one!' So I did a thirty-second piece and put it right after his, and then Tré did one. And so on. We kept connecting them until we had something. I just started getting serious as we went on. We were trying to outdo one another a little bit. A lot of that stuff ended up going into 'Homecoming.' It was just an inspired moment."

> Japanese mini poster for *American Idiot*.

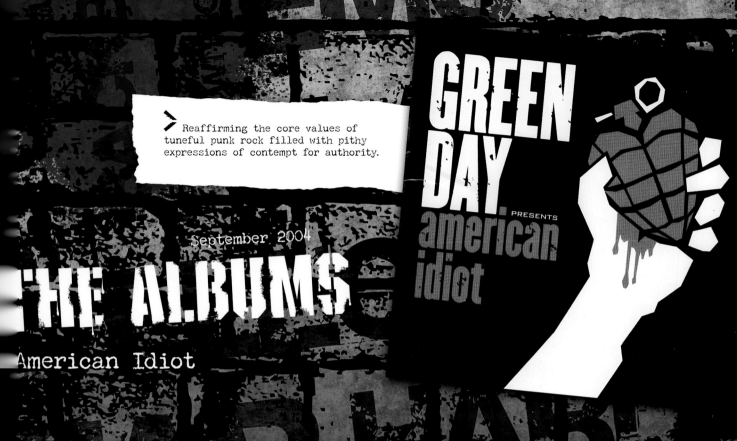

❯ Reaffirming the core values of tuneful punk rock filled with pithy expressions of contempt for authority.

september 2004

THE ALBUMS

American Idiot

At first glance, punk rock and the rock opera might seem to stand at opposite ends of the rock 'n' roll continuum. The rock opera is a long-form genre—one that aims to elevate slashing power chords and clattering handclaps to high art. Punk rock on the other hand is all about short/loud/fast salvos of pure lowbrow rebellion. Militantly unpretentious, its gaze remains fixed at street level.

But there is a common dominator: Punk rock and the rock opera are both based on the assumption that rock 'n' roll has the potential to make large and powerful statements about things that really matter—that it is not a commodity, but the primordial pulse of life itself. Green Day's Billie Joe Armstrong understands this, and from that understanding he fashioned the world's first punk rock opera.

American Idiot is an impressive work by any standard. It contains some of the catchiest, fiercest tunes ever to blast from the amps and traps of Billie Joe, Mike Dirnt, and Tre Cool. Yet it's shot through with colorful characters, arch social observation, evocative symbolism, and recurring motifs (both musical and lyrical) worthy of a master storyteller. *American Idiot* may well be remembered for years to come as the album that defines a supremely screwed-up era.

Armstrong depicts the alarmingly totalitarian tendencies of the Bush II regime as the logical outcome of the vapid disfunction that marked American culture in the decades leading up to the album's 2004 release. Broken homes, Ritalin kids, and shopping mall complacency adorn his "Boulevard of Broken Dreams," for example, while his "Jesus of Suburbia" is crucified not on a cross of pain but on the mind-numbing comfort of a cozy sofa and empty-calorie TV. Armstrong's St. Jimmy—essentially his take on John the Baptist, the Bible's militant zealot prophet—is a dashing yet doomed punk rock hero/avenger. The Magdalene character is Whatsername, whom Armstrong introduces in "She's a Rebel," gender-flipping the Crystals classic.

In one fell and graceful swoop, Billie Joe rescued the Gospel from religious right reactionaries and punk rock from the legions of pop-punk boy bands that had cheapened the p-word. But while *American Idiot* begins in righteous political anger, it ends on a note of personal nostalgia for bygone youth and the reconciliation of rage and love. Like the Who's *Tommy* and *Quadrophenia* before it, Armstrong's rock opera ultimately seems to be about the maturation process.

The rock opera is where great songwriters go when they grow up—after they've conquered the charts, mastered the art of the three-minute pop single, and are ready to tackle a work of epic proportions. It takes a lot of balls to step into this arena, but Billie Joe shouldered the burden of rock history adroitly. Two *American Idiot* selections, "Jesus of Suburbia" and "Homecoming" skillfully revisit Pete Townshend's mid-'60s miniopera structure—a medley of melodic snippets, each of which could be a great song in its own right but are instead segued in rapid fire succession for maximum narrative compression and crazy headlong momentum.

Billie Joe's magnum opus, *American Idiot* is filled with musical quotations, from Johnny Cash to John Lennon, the specter of Spector's "teenage symphonies," the Clash's clarion call, *The Wall*'s looming shadow. This big canvas inspires Dirnt and Cool—arguably the best rhythm section in recent punk—to pummel and thrash with widescreen intensity and mock heroic panache. Nor has Billie Joe let his ambitious songwriting detract from the slamming downstroke solidity of his guitar playing.

The net effect is one that hadn't been felt in some time—the wild exuberance of great rock 'n' roll marshaled as a weapon of resistance.

The lyrics for Dirnt's segment are an exercise in journaling, documenting a boring, lonely day in the studio and falling *asleep while watching Spike TV after ten cups of coffee.* But his forlorn day led him to the emotionally vulnerable refrain—*Nobody likes you, everyone left you/They're all out without you havin' fun*—which would become one of the album's key motifs. Armstrong's and Cool's contributions to "Homecoming" are similarly straightforward snapshots of what was going on in their lives at the time. Billie Joe's "East 12th Street" gives the actual address of the police station where he had to fill out paperwork as part of his community-service obligation. And the soon to be divorced Tré sings *I've got a rock and roll girlfriend, and another ex-wife* in his "Homecoming" entry, "Rock and Roll Girlfriend."

Out of these lightweight autobiographical snippets, Green Day were able to assemble something with more universal resonance, ultimately making "Homecoming" the climactic final act of *American Idiot*'s overall plot line. In form, "Homecoming" and the album's other extended suite, "Jesus of Suburbia," are the direct offspring of pre-*Tommy* mini-operas—"A Quick One While He's Away" and "Rael"—that the Who's Pete Townshend wrote in the mid-'60s. Quite revolutionary in their day, "A Quick One" and "Rael" are both extended rock tracks, each some ten minutes in length and each consisting of a tightly arranged sequence of musical and vocal fragments. Any one of these fragments could have served as a perfect power pop verse, chorus, or bridge, but instead the fragments stay fragmentary and are deployed in a headlong narrative rush. This innovative musical form had fallen into disuse after the '60s, until Green Day revived it on *American Idiot*.

Cobo Hall, Detroit, November 6, 2004. New Found Glory and Sugarcult supported. Both Paul Warner/ WireImage/Getty Images

The *American Idiot* tour on home turf, Bill Graham Civic Auditorium, San Francisco, November 24, 2004. Tim Mosenfelder/Getty Images

"I wanted something that maintains that short attention span thing," Armstrong said, "where it's one great part after another—boom, boom, boom—all put together really well. It's a tricky thing to do. The transitions are really important. With 'Homecoming' and 'Jesus of Suburbia,' we abandoned the conventional verse/chorus/verse/chorus/bridge song structure. And as soon as you open your mind up to this different way of writing, there really are no rules. And once you write something like 'Jesus of Suburbia,' there's no turning back. You have to go ahead and do something serious. It's a scary moment. There's no copping out. If you're going to go down, you're going to go down in flames."

With the song "American Idiot," Green Day had a powerhouse opening for their new album. And Billie Joe sensed that "Homecoming" would work at or near the end, so he proceeded to fill in all the bits in the middle, creating characters and a lightly sketched plot line. The first thing written after "Homecoming" introduces the album's main character, Jesus of Suburbia, who grew directly out of "American Idiot."

"I started thinking, 'Who would be an example of an 'American Idiot?'" Billie Joe explained. "And I came up with 'Jesus of Suburbia.' I wrote the first two lines and it just fit, especially crossing that line between government and religion—fucking with that a bit."

One of the coolest things about *American Idiot*'s biblical subtext is the sly and deft way in which Billie Joe reclaims the Gospels from the Religious Right, radically recontextualizing, creating a sort of punk rock catechism *cum* revolutionary handbook. "I don't know shit about the Bible," he says. "So I wrote my own."

Rehearsing for VH1's *Big in '04*,
Shrine Auditorium, Los Angeles,
November 30, 2004. KMazur/
WireImage/Getty Images

The heroes of traditional rock operas—the Who's Tommy, Pink Floyd's protagonist Pink in *The Wall*—often become messianic figures at some point in their narrative trajectories. But Armstrong's Jesus of Suburbia is an ironic messiah, a powerless Everyman, anesthetized by *television and a steady diet of soda pop and Ritalin.*

"He's an antihero really," Armstrong noted. "But that's what I've always been drawn to. That's the difference between a rock opera and a punk rock opera, I guess. It comes from more of a lower middle-class, suburban kid's perspective."

Which is to say there's a lot of Billie Joe's own story in *American Idiot*. The poignant ballad "Wake Me up When September Ends" addresses the death of Billie Joe's father all those years ago, while the main character's journey from suburbia to the big city reflects Armstrong's own transition from sleepy Rodeo to politicized Berkeley, a rite of passage chronicled in the song "Holiday."

"It's written from the perspective of this kid moving to this really liberal city," says Armstrong, "where there's all these different opinions, and nobody can seem to agree on anything. You have different people on soapboxes. But that song's also about the [Iraq] war too."

Indeed, Armstrong's political rage is at its most virulent in the middle section of "Holiday." It's not hard to decode references to contemporary political figures in lines like, *The representative from California has the floor/Zieg Heil to the President Gasman.*

VH1's *Big in '04*, Shrine Auditorium, Los Angeles, December 1, 2004. John Shearer/ WireImage/Getty Images

"That section of the song is kind of the politicians saying what they really want to say," Billie Joe explained. "One of those giant meetings in Washington. The representative from California gets up and says 'Zieg Heil. Oh my god!' He says, 'Kill all the fags'—using all this language gets people up at arms. But in the end, I tie it into where that shit isn't really my thing."

For all the emotional release that must have come from writing a song like "Holiday" midway through the Bush regime, Billie Joe was also plagued by moments of doubt all the way through the making of *American Idiot*. "Just talking about politics in general is a difficult thing to do," he said. "Because there's a fear, and the fear for me is more about being wrong. Your politics will always change, because your ideas change no matter what."

That humility is one key to *American Idiot*'s enduring appeal. For all their passionate political engagement, Armstrong's musical tirades never lapse into mere dogma. "The album doesn't necessary have an agenda, like telling people what to think," he says. "It's more about trying to find your own individuality. So it was very important to us, when we were writing this, to make sure that it still had that personal side."

In the moments of uncertainty that Armstrong, Dirnt, and Cool faced throughout the making of the album, Rob Cavallo unflaggingly supported them. The band's longtime producer first pointed out the enormous potential in the "Homecoming" suite, and he made sure that Green Day did everything they could to realize that potential.

"Rob was really pushing us, every time that we ever had doubts," said Billie Joe. "And you always have doubts when you make a record like this. There were moments when I thought that people are gonna think we're out of our fucking minds. But whenever that happened, Rob would say, 'No, keep going.' And he would say, 'What if you tried something like this . . .?' And I'd go off in another room and write something. We were just bouncing ideas back and forth like that. So Rob had a huge role—probably more so than any other record we've ever done with him."

As writing for the album unfolded, Jesus of Suburbia became the central figure in an unholy trinity of characters, although the other two personages in the songs are aspects of Jesus of Suburbia's own psyche. On the one hand there's St. Jimmy—swaggering punk rock freedom fighter *par excellence*, charismatic but also somewhat ruthless and nihilistic: *the needle in the vein of the establishment.*

He seems a descendent of some of rock's other Jimmys, such as the mod protagonist in the Who's *Quadrophenia* and the neophyte punk kid who pops up in the bridge of "One Hundred Punks" by Generation X, one of Armstrong's favorite bands. But Billie Joe insists that all of these associations are accidental.

"Jimmy is just one of those names," he says. "It could be Saint James, but it's more of a modern-day name. Like my name's not William, it's Billie. If there's a parallel to *Quadrophenia*, it's the schizophrenic side that the characters have."

Indeed, St. Jimmy's opposite number, as it were, is a girl called Whatsername, introduced in the song "She's a Rebel." The title itself is a riff on the Phil Spector–produced classic "He's a Rebel" by the Crystals, but Billy cites riot grrl grunge band Bikini Kill's "Rebel Girl" as a more immediate inspiration. And indeed Bikini Kill's Kathleen Hanna was drafted to sing the taunting refrain in Dirnt's "Nobody Likes You." There's plenty of '90s riot grrl militancy in the character Whatsername, not to mention echoes of Amanda, the Gilman Street punk rock feminist who jilted Armstrong all those years ago.

And perhaps that's the key to the built-in anonymity in the character's name—she's a shadowy figure from the past. *I remember her face but I can't recall the name*, Billie Joe sings in "Whatsername," the album's retrospective closing track. But the anonymity inherent in this character's name also gives her a sort of revolutionary/populist panache, the face in the crowd—Everywoman, "Mother Revolution," a punk rock counterpart to painter Eugene Delacroix's iconic bare breasted symbol of the French Revolution or the title character of Maxim Gorky's Soviet revolutionary novel *Mother*.

"She's kind of St. Jimmy's nemesis in a lot of ways," says Armstrong. "The constant theme of the record is rage versus love. You can go with the blind rebellion of self-destruction, where St. Jimmy is. But there's also a more love-driven side to that, which is following your beliefs and your ethics. And that's where Jesus of Suburbia really wants to go."

Having completed songwriting for *American Idiot* at Studio 880, Green Day journeyed south to record the album at their familiar Los Angeles haunt, Ocean Way. A project this epic in scope demanded a big sound, and Green Day rose to the occasion. This was not a moment for punk minimalism or Gilman Street "less is more" austerity. Rob Cavallo overdubbed piano parts and Jason Freese was called in to lay down some saxophone tracks, imparting a touch of Springsteen-esque drama. Nor did Billie Joe hesitate to lay on rich layers of guitar tracks, such as the throbbing tremolo electric that floats dreamlike above the solid acoustic rhythm in the soon-to-be megahit "Boulevard of Broken Dreams," or the stark, mosquito-to-a-monster guitar dynamics of the title track.

"It's the most guitar playing I've ever done on a record, I think," said Billie Joe at the time. "I just decided I'm not gonna lay back or anything. If it's time for a solo, I'm gonna play the fucking thing. Whereas in the past I've maybe held back and said, 'Nah, that might sound corny.' But this whole record is sort of about being fifteen and rocking in front of a mirror."

GREEN DAY

BOULEVARD OF BROKEN DREAMS

◄ Adorned with broken homes,
Ritalin kids, and shopping mall
complacency.

With *American Idiot*, Green Day achieved something that previously might have seemed impossible: a graceful yet feisty union of punk rock and classic rock. In the '70s, punk rock arose as the nemesis and antithesis of classic rock. Never, it seemed, would the twain meet, although seasoned rock fans of a certain persuasion had always sensed a kind of continuity. Armstrong was ideally placed along rock history's timeline to articulate that continuity. Equally steeped in contemporary punk culture and rock history, Billie Joe found an ideal precursor in Pete Townshend. The Who had always been the one classic '60s band that was accepted—even revered in some instances—by punk rockers. The vibe of *American Idiot* is much closer to the power chord Mod pop aesthetic of *Quadrophenia* than, say, the rock pomp and circumstance of *The Wall*.

"I've never been into Pink Floyd. Ever," said Billie Joe. "To me Pink Floyd was always the ultimate example of beating around the bush. I'm too impatient to listen to that kind of thing. I mean I have massive respect for Pink Floyd. Without them we couldn't have made a record like [*American Idiot*]. But I've always preferred Townshend. Green Day have always come from that power pop side, whether it's the Who, Cheap Trick, or the Jam. I think the root of pop punk is power pop—that kind of songwriting."

Beyond rock operas or concept albums per se, *American Idiot* is shot through with musical quotations and references to rock's bygone glory days. The historically informed listener will pick up echoes of Springsteen, Bowie, Lennon, and the high drama of Phil Spector's "teenaged symphonies," filtered through the ragged revolutionary grandeur of the Clash's *London Calling*.

"It's great to use classic records like that as references, but nothing more," Armstrong cautioned. "Just because they're all part of that previous generation. For us, *American Idiot* is about taking those classic rock and roll elements, kicking out the rules, putting more ambition in, and making it current. Ambition is the key. Living up to your fullest potential as a songwriter."

Outside the rock arena, musical theater became another source of inspiration. By including these kinds of influences, Billie Joe was unconsciously laying the groundwork for *American Idiot*'s eventual adaptation for the stage. "We listened to *West Side Story*, *The Rocky Horror Picture Show*, *Grease*, and *Jesus Christ Superstar*," Armstrong admitted. "Those were some more references we had, in terms of how to make a record like this."

The September 16, 2004, Los Angeles live debut of *American Idiot* at the Henry Fonda Theater on Sunset Boulevard was certainly rock 'n' roll theater at its very best. The vintage Hollywood theater turned rock palace was packed to its peeling rococo, plaster walls. Paris Hilton—then at seven and a half in her fifteen minutes of fame—was in the house. So was Rancid's Tim Armstrong, who gave the world's first punk rock opera an enthusiastic thumbs-up in the lobby that evening.

Before playing a single note, Green Day elicited a thunderous roar from the crowd. With a second guitarist, keyboardist, and timpani player in tow, Billie Joe was free to play the rock frontman. Arrayed in what would become the *American Idiot* ironic, fascist-drag uniform—tight black shirt and jeans, red tie, tons of eyeliner—Billie Joe mounted the monitors, letting go of his guitar and waving his arms in the air like an electrocuted scarecrow. He introduced a few of the characters as Green Day's new punk rock opera unfolded. But mostly he let the music do the talking.

Which was wise. By the time Green Day powered into the anthemic backbeat finale to "Homecoming," the entire crowd had their hands in the air. For the first time in their lives, many of these listeners were discovering the glorious rush of rock 'n' roll on a grand scale. As if to drive the point home, Green Day encored with a brace of their greatest hits, ending the night with a surprise: a letter perfect rendering of the Queen classic "We Are the Champions." As Green Day's *American Idiot* tour circumnavigated the globe, the band added the Who's "A Quick One While He's Away" to their encore repertoire. *American Idiot* went on to sell more than 14 million copies, garnering a Grammy for Best Rock Album and manifold other signifiers of success and brilliance.

The Punk had met the Godfather, indeed, and the two had become one in the slender, diminutive figure of Billie Joe Armstrong. The "Fat Elvis Period" was now officially over. When I asked about the bloated specter of Billie Joe's former self a few hours before the Henry Fonda debut, Armstrong laughed in his subtly derisive way.

"Yeah, I'm sort of taking better care of myself," he said. "Just getting into running a little bit more. Going on long walks. It's physically therapeutic, and mentally also. I have an excess amount of energy. And you can't always just pick up a forty-ouncer and drink it."

> Rehearsing for the 2004 Billboard Music Awards, MGM Grand Arena, Paradise, Nevada, December 8, 2004. KMazur/ WireImage/Getty Images

chapter **9**

THE SONG OF THE CENTURY

The sweet smell of success is invariably undercut by a faint, acrid whiff of mortality. Success is by nature impermanent and fleeting. Even when riding high, there's always a little anxiety over maintaining the ride's momentum, if not an outright fear of crashing. This was where Green Day found themselves in the glowing aftermath of *American Idiot*. They'd pioneered a brave new rock genre, making one of the most important rock albums of the fledgling new century—and one that could stand tall alongside the great rock albums of the previous century. Armstrong, Dirnt, and Cool had certainly ridden the momentum of that triumph, crisscrossing the world playing to sold-out audiences and releasing the live CD/DVD set *Bullet in a Bible* in 2005. Green Day had also regained the rights to their early albums in 2005, owing to nonpayment of royalties from Lookout!, and would ultimately reissue them on Reprise. They'd firmly secured their legacy.

The sweet smell of success undercut
by a faint whiff of mortality.
Mercer Hotel, New York City, May 15,
2009. AP Photo/Bruce Gilbert

▲ London's burning. Carling
Academy Brixton, January 25, 2005.
Jo Hale/Getty Images

But inevitably they had to settle down and start work on the successor to *American Idiot*. This new album would take three-plus years, working on and off, to complete. As the band commenced work on the record in early 2006, their position was analogous to where they'd been after *Dookie* became massive. Once again, they faced the daunting pressure of following up a blockbuster, career-defining album. Only now they were far more seasoned. They'd been through the cycle of career ups and downs a few times and come out both tougher and better able to negotiate the tricky crosscurrents of creativity and the ever-shifting pop culture zeitgeist.

"There's pressure every time there's a success like *American Idiot*," said Billy Joe. "But what do you do with that pressure? Do you let it get the best of you, or do you use it as some kind of fuel? So I think we were just trying to rise off the shoulders of *American Idiot* and keep moving forward as songwriters."

BRIT Awards, Earls Court,
London, February 9, 2005. © Toby
Melville/Reuters/Corbis

Where the success of *Dookie* had been something of an embarrassment to Armstrong and his band mates, who were uneasy at being seen as traitors to their Gilman Street, anti-commercial ideals, the afterglow of *American Idiot* found Green Day much more comfortable with the fame they'd achieved, and thus better able to progress artistically.

"*American Idiot* made me much more accepting that being a rock star is a good thing," Billie Joe said. "We come from an era where 'rock star' was the worst thing somebody could have been called. But I think we've all just become more accepting of the fact that this success is a great opportunity. So let's have fun with it. I think it changed my life to where I'm having more fun than I ever had before. I'm trying to think if there's anything bad about success . . . but I don't think there is anything bad about it!"

And so Green Day started putting new songs together for the album that would become *21st Century Breakdown*. "I think the first song we wrote was 'Mass Hysteria,'" Armstrong recalled. "And then 'Know Your Enemy' came up a couple of songs later. And from there it went to '21 Guns.'"

Once again Armstrong found himself writing songs of protest and social conscience, triggered by the crisis state of American society, now in the second presidential term of George W. Bush. By the time "Mass Hysteria" was written, the undercurrent of paranoia that Billie Joe had slyly chided during the *Warning* era had erupted through the surface and left the American landscape scarred by polarizing extremism, xenophobia, and corporate greed that left less and less for all but the fortunate few. Once again, Billie wasn't afraid to muster the proverbial "three chords and the truth," unflinchingly depicting the mood of the times: *Red Alert is the color of panic/Elevated to the point of static/Getting in the hearts of the fanatics/And the neighborhood's a loaded gun.*

While Armstrong soon realized that perhaps he was writing another rock opera, the overall mood of the emerging work was distinct from *American Idiot*. Where *American Idiot* encapsulated the rage that many felt at the Bush ascendancy following a historically shady election, *21st Century Breakdown* would capture the mood of entrenched despair that marked the second half of the Bush regime, when the effects of that administration's laissez faire, corporate-friendly, environment-hostile policies had wrought economic and ecological disaster, leaving the poor, working, and middle classes struggling to survive.

"It's a different crisis every week, especially since 2005," Billie Joe lamented. "Natural disasters, the environment is fucked up, the automotive industry is taking a dive, there are economic bailouts, a financial crisis, and two wars that we're still fighting."

Billie Joe had taken to writing songs on piano as well as guitar, the deep tonal range and drama of the former instrument also lending to *21st Century Breakdown*'s overall mood of gravitas. "I kind of taught myself how to play piano, and Jason Freese also taught me just a little bit," Armstrong said. "I don't even know how to play and sing at the same time yet. But the piano kind of changed my writing a little bit. It leads you to different chord progressions and just kind of opens you up a little bit. . . . So 'Last Night on Earth,' 'Restless Heart Syndrome,' and '21 Guns' were written on piano. Things like that."

> Punk rock flash pots at
the 47th Annual Grammy Awards,
Staples Center, Los Angeles,
February 13, 2005. Timothy A.
Clary/AFP/Getty Images

∨ Concert T-shirt, circa 2005.
WycoVintage.com

For the first time since their pre-Reprise career, Green Day were making an album completely without the involvement of Rob Cavallo. Their longtime producer wasn't even on board in an advisory role, as he'd been on *Warning*. "Rob was sort of going his way and we were going ours," Billy Joe simply said, "and it wasn't really making sense to work with him on this one. I think we owed it to ourselves as artists to go and work with other people. I mean I wouldn't count out working with Rob again, but he just wasn't the right guy for this record."

However, Green Day did still find themselves in need of an outside perspective to help shape their material. They considered working with tunesmith and producer Linda Perry, who'd collaborated with everyone from Christina Aguilera and Pink to Cheap Trick and Courtney Love. But they ultimately threw their lot in with Butch Vig, a key architect of the alternative '90s sound through his production work on iconic albums like Nirvana's *Nevermind* and the Smashing Pumpkins' *Melon Collie and the Infinite Sadness*. Ironically, Green Day had once been contemptuous of the grunge sound with its big fuzzy guitar sounds invariably processed through Big Muff distortion pedals. But they nonetheless found a kindred spirit in Vig, who also shared Green Day's passion for power pop and punk sounds.

Rod Laver Arena, Melbourne.
March 10, 2005. © Martin Philbey
ZUMA/Corbis

"I think we were at a point where we were driving ourselves crazy with the songwriting, says Armstrong. "And we said, 'OK, now it's time to bring in an outside perspective.' We only met a couple of people. . . . I knew Butch was capable of making a great record. But it was more about how we related to each other and if we liked each other, really. And I liked him immediately. He just brought a sense of calm and class. I never really knew always what he was doing and when he was tweaking out on things. He's a very techie guy. He can geek out on something for a long time. But on hearing the end result, I think we managed to hit a top end, a low end, and overall sonic quality that I don't think we ever really achieved before."

Perhaps what Vig shared most with Green Day was a maverick spirit and general indifference to the methods and received wisdom of the mainstream music industry. "The thing I liked about Butch is that he's always followed his own taste," said Billie Joe. "He wanted to make records that he liked. It's like he was recording with peers, and he's not the kind of person who goes for the money. Or goes for what's gonna give him that big hit. He wants to make it sound great and all."

Vig played the traditional producer's role of spotting potential gems amid heaps of raw material and encouraging the band to polish those gems to perfection. "I'd kind of forgotten about the song 'Horseshoes and Handgrenades,'" says Billie Joe. "As a songwriter, you sometimes lose perspective on songs because you're so close to them. You start taking certain songs for granted. But Butch was like 'We're recording that goddamned song!' And then I showed him the melody for 'Restless Heart Syndrome.' It's weird the way you sometimes start a song, but don't finish it. With that song I was kind of like, 'Oh, I'll just wait and record it five years from now.' But Butch was like, 'No, no, no. You gotta chase down that melody now, and you gotta find those lyrics.'"

Vig also helped Armstrong and the band bring the big picture into sharper focus. "I started throwing around ideas of how I wanted the record to be," Billie Joe recollected. "And Butch threw in a couple of ideas. I think one thing he came up with was the phrase 'rebel songs.' 'Cause, looking at the material, there's a lot of rebel songs. There's 'Know Your Enemy,' for example, which is a big fat rebel song.'"

American Idiot tour, San Francisco and Carson, California.

▲ Postcard for canceled
American Idiot tour date, 2005.

▲ Released in November 2005,
Bullet in a Bible culled tracks
from the band's two-night stand
at England's Milton Keynes
National Bowl the previous June.

"Know Your Enemy" is also a textbook Green Day classic, starting with a huge thwacking drum beat (killer drum sounds being one of Vig's fortés), leading the way into a full force punk rock call to arms. The lyric echoes John Lydon's "anger is an energy" mantra from Public Image's "Rise." Consummate rebels both, Armstrong and Lydon point to the truth that the real revolution starts not on the streets but in the individual heart and mind. The real enemy is one's own indifference. *Silence is the enemy*, as Armstrong's song declares.

"I think it's anything from within," said Billie Joe of the enemy's larger identity. "For me, it's just about trying to keep a spark of vitality—what I learned from punk rock—and sticking to your guns. But also wanting to learn something new, and not getting distracted by television addiction. Trying to read between the lines of the lies that come at you. The song says *rally up the demons of your soul*. Just try to have a sense of urgency about yourself."

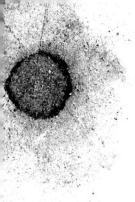

Static is one of the *21st Century Breakdown*'s key motifs. Indeed the first sound heard on the album is the white noise crackle of a radio being tuned—an audio phenomenon that recurs at several key points on the album. Static—the sound and the word itself—becomes a powerful signifier for one of the central issues in early twenty-first-century life: the disorienting and often dispiriting effect of the broadband information explosion, be it calculated propaganda masquerading as television news or the sheer avalanche of 95-percent-pure digital manure that belches out of electronic devices on a daily basis.

"It think it comes at you from all angles," Armstrong said. "CNN is just as responsible for confusing people as Fox News. The thing is to get past all the bullshit and noises in your own head. Just try turning the noise down and find some power in silence. This is a strange time. It seems like less kids want to be rock stars. They want to be the next guy who invents YouTube or Twitter or something."

The static motif comes across most directly in "The Static Age." "It's about how you're just bombarded with information," Billie Joe noted. "They come up with new diseases to have, that you then need to be medicated for. It's like graffiti in the sky, or useless advertising in the sky. Like you're taking away a chunk of the sky to sell me something. It just gets overwhelming. And the song is overwhelming."

Like *American Idiot*, *21st Century Breakdown* is largely composed of song suites. But on the latter album, Armstrong moved away from the amphetamine manic compression of the Townshend-inspired mini-opera, wherein five or six song fragments get packed into one composition. Instead, he created more spacious musical forms that folded only two or three song ideas into a more expansive kind of suite. Clearly Billie Joe was finding his own unique expression of the mini-opera legacy. *21st Century Breakdown*'s title track is a perfect case in point.

"I had '21st Century Breakdown' as a demo version," Armstrong explained, "just a four-track. And we had this whole other song, 'Class of 13,' with an Irish kind of part in it. Those were two completely different songs, but I said 'Look, if I drop the key to "21st Century Breakdown" and put it together with that other song, it could work.' And I realized that that's kind of what the whole record is about—breaking down a moment in time to try to make sense of it. And literally it's like a nervous breakdown, but also a societal breakdown. So I said, 'Maybe we should go for that.' And Butch Vig said, 'Yeah, that sounds great!'"

Regarded as unlucky in Western culture, the number 13 has also become the adoptive numeral of punk rockers and other societal outcasts, a black badge of courage borne as a tattoo or worn as an emblem. But for Armstrong and Cool, the number carries an even more personal significance. "The class of 2013 is when my son and Tré's daughter are going to be graduating high school," Billie Joe said. "I just thought, 'Wow, what an unfortunate year to graduate—but also what a cool year. I wouldn't mind wearing a t-shirt saying Class of '13.' So I just started thinking about the Generation Zero, born under a bad sign. Maybe we're all part of the Class of '13 right now. And it can also be like the name of the band that's playing. Instead of Green Day maybe we could call ourselves the Class of '13."

Green Day and U2 joined forces to help reopen the New Orleans Superdome after Hurricane Katrina. The two bands performed before the New Orleans Saints-Atlanta Falcons football game on September 25, 2006. Soul Brother/FilmMagic/Getty Images

U2 AND GREEN DAY

THE SAINTS ARE COMING

> U2 and Green Day's Rick Rubin-produced cover of Scottish punk band the Skids helped raise money for musicians affected by Hurricane Katrina. The live B-side got mixing and arranging help from legendary producer Bob Ezrin, while photographer Anton Corbijn pitched in for the sleeve photography.

With the couplet *My generation is zero/I never made it as a working class hero*, "21st Century Breakdown" evokes both Pete Townshend's "My Generation" and John Lennon's "Working Class Hero," two of greatest outsider rebel songs in the entire rock canon. But Billie Joe puts a negative spin on both references. His generation is *not* the blessed mod-cum-hippie children of the '60s who ushered in civil rights, the sexual revolution, and consciousness expansion, halting the Vietnam War and bringing Nixon to his knees. To cite a popular saying of the time, the '90s were the '60s upside down. Consciously rejecting the '60s, many punk rockers pride themselves on their lack of utopian ideals. But as a true son of the doctrinaire, proactive Bay Area/Gilman Street incarnation of punk, Armstrong has never been comfortable with utter, bleak nihilism.

21st Century Breakdown, like its predecessor, is rife with quotes from the glorious classic rock past. "Last of the American Girls" echoes Tom Petty's "American Girl," albeit as through a glass darkly. The anthemic "21 Guns" is a direct melodic riff on Mott the Hoople's "All the Young Dudes." Some of these references might be unconscious on Armstrong's part, and most of them surely sail right over the heads of younger Green Day fans. But it's not like Armstrong is plagiarizing; he's a gifted enough tunesmith and lyricist to come up with killer hooks of his own in great abundance. Rather, he seems to plead a heartfelt case that the rock music of his time can still change the world, that it remains an enormously powerful thing. He deliberately invokes the glorious past in order to point the way to an equally glorious future. There is something genuinely heroic in his efforts to make rock something that matters once again, even in the age of digital downloads.

"Why do I do it?" he once replied to an interview question. "Because it's art! It's an art form. It's just something that I feel I have to do. That I've always wanted to do. I love great albums—anything from *Revolver* to *Dark Side of the Moon* to *London Calling*. I like making records where the songs speak to each other and that also have some great singles in there too. I've got nothing against singles. But I love the art of making albums."

Out of Armstrong's songwriting process for *21st Century Breakdown*, two central characters emerged. Christian and Gloria are two lovers trying to make a life for themselves in the dysfunctional, economically depressed, and consummately fucked-up early-twenty-first-century America.

"I've always loved the name Gloria," says Armstrong. "And Christian, that's just an interesting name. It's like St. Jimmy. Christian is a Christian name for sure. So it's another way of playing with words. I think if there's one positive person you could pull out of the record, it's Gloria. Because she's the person who wants to carry the torch and declare her own independence and sense of worth in punk rock and in living a life that might be a bit more subterranean. And Christian, his torch is more about burning the place down—self-destructive. So there's a yin and yang between the two."

But the characters and the plot of *21st Century Breakdown* seem a little less clearly delineated than the dramatis personae and mise en scène of *American Idiot*. In fact, Billie Joe has gone so far as to say that *21st Century Breakdown* has no plot or characters at all.

"There's not a linear story throughout the whole record," he said. "I would say that the linear thing about the record is the music. I think the characters Christian and Gloria symbolize something. They reflect something about the songs. They're in there just as iconic symbolism of two people trying to live in this era. So the album doesn't become all political. There are love songs in there too."

Ultimately, the tension between Christian and Gloria represents Armstrong's own conflicting personality traits—his engaged idealism perpetually at odds with his nihilistic streak.

"I'm singing my own personal experience through both of them," he admitted. "I just like to add names to give the characters flesh and blood. I think, in a way, that makes it a little less self-indulgent. Less about me. So people can maybe have their own attachment."

Before diving into *American Idiot*, Green Day had cleared the air and loosened up by getting involved in the Network project. With *21st Century Breakdown*, the band took their break three-quarters of the way through, in late 2007 and early 2008, suspending work on the album to knock out a quick and dirty album of British Invasion/garage rock scorchers under the pseudonym the Foxboro Hot Tubs.

The resultant album, *Stop, Drop and Roll!!!!* is a blast from start to finish, not to mention a blast from the past. The album cover's design echoes the formulaic album packaging of the mid-'60s. (Although one wonders about the Satanic logo in the upper right-hand corner of the rear cover. Perhaps another move to piss off the religious right?) The disc itself is done up like a miniature 45 rpm single from the '60s. The whole album is a loving homage to one of Armstrong's favorite musical eras and enduring songwriting inspirations.

"That album was just a shitload of alcohol and an eight-track recorder," Billie Joe said. "We had this Tascam unit with a [quarter-inch] reel-to-reel recorder inside the actual mixing board. It was something that was made in the early '80s or something. We just went in, we had all this vintage gear, and we just started riffing. I love all that old garage rock, so we just went for it and had a good time. We went on tour for the album and we drank way too much and we were just having a great time together. I think we needed that escape for a little while to refuel us, or bring us together more."

The band took a break from the recording of *21st Century Breakdown* to knock out a quick and dirty album of British Invasion/garage rock scorchers under the pseudonym the Foxboro Hot Tubs.

Green Day returned to *21st Century Breakdown* with renewed energy, and the album ultimately took the form of three extended musical suites: "Heroes and Cons," "Charlatans and Saints," and "Horseshoes and Handgrenades." Each is packed with some of Armstrong's best and most diverse songwriting. Two tracks, "Peacemaker" and "¡Viva La Gloria! (Little Girl)," reprise the jaunty Eastern European feel of "Misery" from *Warning*.

"I think I was discouraged from that sound for a while," says Armstrong. "But those songs just came out naturally, which was cool. They definitely have that gypsy punk kind of thing going on."

"After the Lobotomy" is another ambitious track. "It starts with this acoustic ballad thing and then turns into a completely different song," Armstrong explained. "Then it goes back to the original acoustic ballad thing, but done in a gushing, power chord way. I love messing with arrangements and seeing how they ebb and flow."

GREEN DAY

21ST CENTURY BREAKDOWN

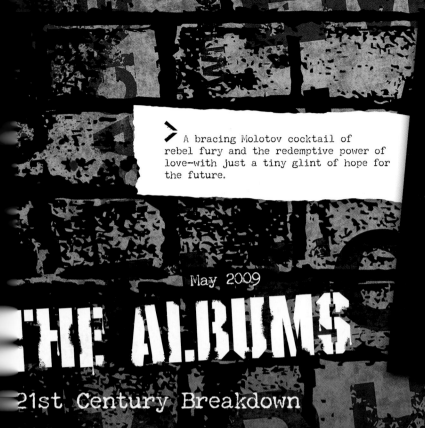

> A bracing Molotov cocktail of rebel fury and the redemptive power of love—with just a tiny glint of hope for the future.

May 2009

THE ALBUMS

21st Century Breakdown

'm not fucking arou-ou-ound!

Billie Joe Armstrong's strident, angry voice ears out of the speakers with an urgency hat makes you think the man himself is about o rip through the grille cloth and personally hrottle all the corporate criminals, talk-radio creeps, hypocrite politicians, Bible-thumping varmongers, and greed-drunk oppressors who have reduced the United States of America, and indeed the entire world, to its present sorry state. The song is called "Horseshoes and Handgrenades" and it's one of eighteen glorious tracks on Green Day's *21st Century Breakdown*.

The brilliant follow-up to the band's 2005 punk rock opera tour de force, *American Idiot*, *21st Century Breakdown* traces the fortunes of a young couple, Christian and Gloria, as they try to make a life for themselves in an America where opportunities have become thin on the ground for the working and middle classes and the poor—the whole great mass of humanity not among the well-heeled haves and have mores favored by the administration that was leaving power just as *21st Century Breakdown* hit the stores and charts.

The plot line is even fuzzier than *American Idiot*'s sketchy narrative, but the emotions

are powerfully clear. For all the album's impassioned political context, Billie Joe's focus is essentially personal. He tells his tale of recent world events in terms of their human cost. "Last Night on Earth" is the love letter that every soldier in harm's way wishes that he or she could write and send back home. The album's slashing first single, "Know Your Enemy," could target any number of public figures. Instead, Armstrong tells us that the ultimate enemy lies within—in our own complacency, indifference, or unwillingness to get involved and make the world a better place. When all is said and done, *21st Century Breakdown* is a rallying cry for an inner revolution. And that's why it will continue to resonate even after the current sociopolitical morass has long since faded into history.

On the subject of history, *21st Century Breakdown*, like its predecessor, is deeply steeped in rock's rich legacy. There are melodic and lyrical references to everyone from John Lennon and Pete Townshend to Mott the Hoople and Tom Petty. Armstrong and the band temper the infectious melodicism of their power pop forebears with the sweeping grandeur of '70s classic rock and punk's fuck-all belligerence. This ambitious invocation

of the rock pantheon might not work so well were it not turbocharged by Green Day's combined musical muscle. Armstrong has dialed in his guitar attack with deadly precision, deploying punk rock downstrokes, power chord clangor, and richly melodic leads in all the right proportions. Meanwhile, bassist Mike Dirnt and drummer Tré Cool remain one of the most formidable rhythm sections in current rock. Solid yet nimble bass lines crisscross drumming that is a dizzying amalgam of tight control and manic energy.

As musicians and songwriters, Green Day have evolved steadily since the heady days of the mid-'90s when they ignited the pop punk explosion with albums like *Dookie* and *Nimrod*. *21st Century Breakdown* is a stimulating tonic for troubled times—a bracing Molotov cocktail of rebel fury and the redemptive power of love, laced with just a tiny glint of hope for the future. In the four years following the release of *American Idiot*, fans wondered if Green Day could ever top—or even equal— that groundbreaking work. On *21st Century Breakdown*, they make this monumental task look easy.

goldenvoice presents

GREEN DAY

and jimmy eat world • oct 8th w/ against me • oct 9th w/ flogging molly • 2005

at the home depot center in the city of lost angels

McPherson

* art by tara mcpherson, in her own world • printed at diesel fuel prints, on planet earth • www.taramcpherson.com • www.dieselfuelprints.com •

The song might be taken as an indictment of the dumbing down of American culture—what rapper and activist Chuck D notably called "The Dumb-Assification of America"—but "After the Lobotomy" actually had a more humble origin.

"I got the title from a headline in the *San Francisco Chronicle*," Billy Joe recounted. "The article was about this guy who'd written a book about how he'd gotten a lobotomy because his father thought he was too hyperactive. He was a problem child or something, so his father made him get a lobotomy. So sure, the song could be about the dumbing down of society, but it all comes from personal experience you know!"

Work on *21st Century Breakdown* had begun deep in the grim darkness of the Bush II years. Fittingly for the mood of those times, the album begins with a sort of eulogy ("Song of the Century" later reprised as "American Eulogy"). *Tell me a story into that goodnight*, Armstrong sings in a spectral voice, echoing Dylan Thomas's famous poem, "Go Not Gentle into That Good Night," with its well-known exhortation to *rage, rage against the dying of the light*. Green Day had certainly done plenty raging over the course of *21st Century Breakdown*'s 69-plus minutes.

> A textbook Green Day classic, starting with a huge thwacking drum beat leading the way into a full force punk rock call to arms.

A. 21 GUNS*
B. FAVORITE SON**

*Produced by Butch Vig & Green Day / Engineered by Chris Dugan / Mixed by Chris Lord-Alge
**Produced by Rob Cavallo and Green Day / Engineered and Mixed by Doug McKean
Words by Billie Joe. Music by Green Day. WB Music Corp./Green Daze Music Administered by WB Music Corp. ASCAP

BILLIE JOE ARMSTRONG — LEAD VOCALS, GUITAR
MIKE DIRNT — BASS, BACKING VOCALS
TRÉ COOL — DRUMS

Management: Pat Magnarella, PMC / Art Direction and Design: Chris Bilheimer

*FROM THE REPRISE ALBUM 21ST CENTURY BREAKDOWN

21ST CENTURY
BREAKDOWN

GREENDAY.COM
Reprise Records, A Warner Music Group Comp...
4694, 1290 Avenue Of The Americas, New Yo...
for the U.S. and WEA International Inc. for the...
hiring, lending, public performance and broadcas...
LC14666. W817.

> The direct riff on Mott the Hoople's "All the Young Dudes" might be unconscious on Armstrong's part.

Special Idiot Club show, Bowery
Ballroom, New York City, May 18, 2009.
Both KMazur/WireImage/Getty Images

7 Maybe they drank too much
Coca-Cola. MTV Video Music Awards
Japan, Super Arena, Saitama,
Japan, May 30, 2009. Jun Sato/
WireImage/Getty Images

But as work on the album was completed in the spring of 2009, a new light seemed to kindle across America, as the nation's first African-American president, Barack Obama, took office. There was a sense of hope, albeit guarded, that he would undo some of his predecessor's more pernicious policies. It seemed that what was to come had to be at least a little better than what had gone before.

This mood of fragile optimism is perfectly captured in *21st Century Breakdown*'s closing track, "See the Light," with its refrain *I just wanna see the light*. Armstrong notably doesn't say he *sees* the light. Just that it would sure be nice if he—and presumably all of us—could. "We finally got rid of—thank God!—this president and this administration that was pretty responsible for all the shit that was going on," Billie Joe said. "So there's anxiety about how everything has gotten fucked up in the last six to eight years. But there's also this sense of hope, together with a fear of what's going to happen in the future, because the future is unwritten. It's unclear. And I think a lot of that is reflected in the album, especially when you come to the conclusion and the song 'See the Light.' That song is a different kind of call to arms than 'Know Your Enemy.' It's an inner call to arms, almost a spiritual call to arms. As a songwriter, you're trying to find the truth with every song you're writing. And I think with 'See the Light,' the truth there is, 'Oh *fuck* yeah. I just wanna be happy.'"

GREEN DAY
with FRANZ FERDINAND
August 8, 2009 | Toyota Center | Houston, TX

Green Day

Special Guest:
KAISER CHIEFS

AUG 5, 2009
Amway Arena
Orlando

BUY TICKETS AT LIVENATION.COM
SCOTTYBALDWIN.COM   IRON FORGE PRESS .COM
LIVE NATION

Arco Arena, Sacramento,
California, August 24, 2009.
Tim Mosenfelder/Getty Images

Artist: Ivan Minsloff/
ivanminsloff.com

The *American Idiot* tour continues. Chula Vista, California, 2005.

Screened just once—
at Grauman's Egyptian
Theatre in Hollywood on
March 25, 2009—*Heart Like a
Hand Grenade* documented the
band during the recording
of American Idiot.

While *21st Century Breakdown* didn't sell as well as *American Idiot*—achieving platinum
status in the United States compared with *Idiot*'s five times platinum, with proportionate
results internationally—Armstrong, Dirnt, and Cool still had plenty to be happy about. They
had created two epic, landmark works in fairly rapid succession—a rare accomplishment
in the rock arena. August predecessors like the Who and Pink Floyd had released smaller-
scale, single albums in between double-album narrative blockbusters like *Tommy* and
Quadrophenia or *Dark Side of the Moon* and *The Wall*. Moreover, numerous songs from both
American Idiot and *21st Century Breakdown* had embedded themselves deeply in rock culture.
When historians of the future look back on the first decade of the twenty-first century, they
will surely cite lyrics from Green Day's two sprawling rock narratives.

But it seemed clear that Armstrong was building toward something even bigger. As soon
as *21st Century Breakdown* was completed, he began to speculate about possible ways to
combine the album's plot and characters with those of *American Idiot*. "I always thought it
would be cool if we could make a movie with Jesus of Suburbia, St. Jimmy, Whatsername,
Gloria, and Christian," he said. "Like combining two records together."

The wheels would soon be set in motion for this grand vision to be realized.

Released in November 2009, Last Night on Earth: Live in Tokyo featured performances recorded the previous May at that city's Akasaka BLITZ.

S.E.C.C., Glasgow, October 19, 2009. Ross Gilmore/Redferns/Getty Images

BROADWAY AND BEYOND

The great rock operas tend to combine the themes of youthful disillusionment and anger with the inherent energy and exuberance of youth. These are universal emotions, shared by people in all time periods. For this reason, rock operas, like their classical counterparts, tend to be evergreen. They lend themselves to repeated revivals in a variety of media, settings, and contexts. Townshend's *Tommy* and *Quadrophenia* have successfully found their way onto the stage and screen. *The Wall* became a film very soon after being released as an album.

So it was pretty much a no-brainer for director Michael Mayer to come up with the idea of turning *American Idiot* into a stage musical. He approached Green Day, who agreed to the collaboration. Armstrong had long ago confessed a fondness for musical dramas like *West Side Story*, and Green Day had long since abandoned any punk rock qualms they may once have entertained about embracing so bourgeois an art form as the stage musical.

Fairly early on, the idea emerged to draft Green Day songs outside of *American Idiot* into the show, and many of these songs would come from *21st Century Breakdown*, whose relatively amorphous plot seemed to facilitate its absorption in *American Idiot*. A brand-new song, "When It's Time," was crafted for the production as well.

Backstage during the final
American Idiot soundcheck, St.
James Theatre, New York City,
March 23, 2010. KMazur/WireImage/
Getty Images

▲ *21st Century Breakdown* takes on Southeast Asia.

➤ Paris, France, 2010.

Taking the red carpet at the 64th
Annual Tony Awards, Radio City Music
Hall, New York City, June 13, 2010.
Jeremy Kost/WireImage/Getty Images

Mayer also expanded the original cast of characters, endowing Jesus of Suburbia (also known as Johnny in the work) with two male friends, Will and Tunny, each of whom has a girlfriend, Heather and the Extraordinary Girl, respectively. The producer didn't draft Christian and Gloria from *21st Century Breakdown* directly into *American Idiot*'s stage incarnation, as Billie Joe had originally envisioned. But the troubled trajectory of Will and Heather's relationship parallels the trials of Christian and Gloria's romance in many ways. And Tunny's narrative, which includes military service and serious injury in the line of duty, seems born of the lyric to "Last Night on Earth." Meanwhile, the Extraordinary Girl—the nurse who treats Tunny in his recovery and falls in love with him—seems imbued with the saintly, if fiery, redemptive qualities of many Armstrong heroines.

The stage adaptation of *American Idiot* debuted on September 4, 2009, at the Berkeley Repertory Theater and ran through November 15, generally garnering rave reviews and an enthusiastic response from audiences. It is fitting that this new chapter in Green Day's career began in the radical college town from which they'd first launched themselves some two decades earlier. Almost inevitably, though, the production moved on to Broadway, debuting at the St. James Theatre on March 24, 2010.

The Broadway production of *American Idiot* didn't stint on pure rock power. A very competent pit band was fully amped up and unafraid to interpret Green Day's music in the true punk rock sprit with which it had been written. Nor did the show's producers hold back financially. The Broadway production reportedly cost somewhere between eight and ten million dollars to mount.

Ticket sales surged dramatically when Billie Joe Armstrong himself assumed the role of St. Jimmy—Jesus of Suburbia's dangerous alter ego—from September 28 through October 3, 2010. He reprised the role some fifty more times in early 2011. Later in the year, singer-songwriter Melissa Etheridge and AFI frontman Davey Havok also played St. Jimmy. February 2011 also saw the launch of a touring production. When all was said and done, the show would win six Tony Awards, along with much critical and popular acclaim. The cast soundtrack album won the 2011 Grammy for Best Musical Show Album.

Plans for a film adaptation of the play got underway in 2010 when Tom Hanks's production company, Playtone, optioned the musical version of *American Idiot*. It seems likely that the film version of *American Idiot* will be released in 2013 through Universal Pictures, with Michael Mayer as director and Dustin Lance Black as screenwriter. There is much speculation as to whether Billie Joe Armstrong will once again play the lead role.

> Dirnt has described his Adeline-released side project the Frustrators as sounding "like a cross between Blondie and the Rezillos."

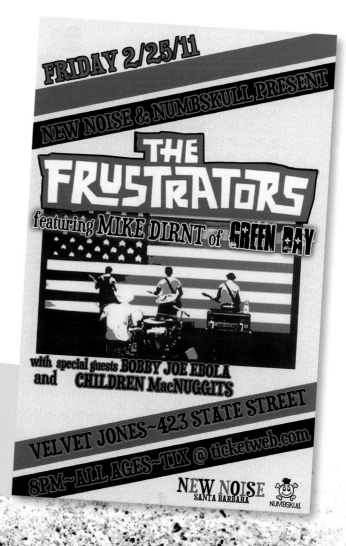

21st Century Breakdown tour,
Comfort Dental Amphitheater, Denver,
August 28, 2010. © Scott D. Smith/Corbis

Meanwhile, early in 2012, they entered the studio to record another ambitious project, described by Green Day as a trilogy comprising LPs entitled *¡Uno!*, *¡Dos!*, and *¡Tre!*, with Rob Cavallo once again at the production helm. The LPs, it was announced, would be released separately, in September and November 2012, and January 2013.

Taken together, *American Idiot* and *21st Century Breakdown* certainly feel like the first two-thirds of an epic trilogy. Now it looks like the third installment of that trilogy will be a trilogy in its own right. Will Billie Joe go *Quadrophenia* one better and write a whole album based on each member of Green Day? The three radio stations always playing inside his head certainly seem to be broadcasting at full bandwidth.

Soundcheck at New Meadowlands Stadium, East Rutherford, New Jersey, September 13, 2010. The band was joined onstage by the cast of *American Idiot* prior to the New York Jets' 2010 opener.
Al Pereira/WireImage/Getty Images

"We are at the most prolific and creative time in our lives" said Green Day in an April 12, 2012, press release. "This is the best music we've ever written, and the songs just keep coming. Instead of making one album, we are making a three-album trilogy. Every song has the power and energy that represents Green Day on all emotional levels. We just can't help ourselves. . . . We are going epic as fuck!"

It seems a pretty safe bet that Green Day will continue to make great music for quite some time. Their history has always been fairly light on tales of dysfunction or in-band fighting. After all these years, the three genuinely seem to like each other.

"Mike, Tré, and I were hanging out with Lars from Metallica the other night," Billie Joe said. "And he was like, 'Man, I can't believe that you guys are such good friends! I just can't believe it.' And I was like, 'Well that kind of goes without saying. Isn't it supposed to be like that?' We may not do cartwheels through the fields together like in *A Hard Day's Night*. But we have grown up together—literally."

▲ Early in 2012, the band entered the studio to record a trilogy comprising LPs entitled *¡Uno!*, *¡Dos!*, and *¡Tre!*, with Rob Cavallo once again at the production helm.

▼ The Rock and Roll Hall of Fame induction ceremony, Public Hall, Cleveland, Ohio, April 14, 2012. The band was on hand to induct Guns 'N' Roses. Jeff Kravitz/ FilmMagic/Getty Images

Deepest gratitude to my beloved wife, Robin, for her invaluable assistance with research, discography compilation, copyediting, and proofreading, and for her perspicacious critiques of the work in progress. This book would not have been possible without her. Thanks also to my editor, Dennis Pernu, for excellent advice, input, and guidance. I am indebted to my *Guitar World* magazine colleague Richard Bienstock for recommending me as author of this book, and to my longtime friend, *Guitar World* editor-in-chief Brad Tolinski, for much support over the years, and for assigning me all of the Green Day feature interview articles that form the basis of this work.

While my own interviews with Green Day form the primary source for this book, Mark Spitz's excellent Green Day bio, *Nobody Likes You*, was an important secondary resource, as were the info-packed Green Day fan website geekstinkbreath.net and Warner Bros.' well-crafted series of press kits for Green Day album releases, which contain statements by key players from the band's salad days, such as Lawrence Livermore and Ben Weasel, proving that Green Day never forget their own! My thanks also go to Masters of the PR Universe Brian Bumbury and Mitch Schneider for facilitating my Green Day interviews over the years so flawlessly.

Finally, supreme gratitude to Billy Joe Armstrong, Mike Dirnt, and Tré Cool for still caring about rock 'n' roll and creating music that lives up to the genre's very highest standards.

—Alan di Perna 2012

MBI Publishing Company titles are also available at discounts in bulk quantity for industrial
or sales-promotional use. For details write to Special Sales Manager at MBI Publishing Company,
400 First Avenue North, Suite 300, Minneapolis, MN, 55401 USA

ISBN: 978-0-7603-4324-1

Library of Congress Cataloging-in-Publication Data

Di Perna, Alan, 1953-
  Green Day : the unauthorized illustrated history / by Alan di Perna.
     p. cm.
  Includes index.
    ISBN 978-0-7603-4324-1
  1. Green Day (Musical group) 2. Punk rock musicians–United States–Biography. I. Title.
  ML421.G74D5 2012
  782.42166092'2–dc23
  [B]
                                    2012012516

Page 1: London, January 2005. *Nigel Crane/Redferns/Getty Images*
Page 2: Parts unknown, circa 1994. © *Pictorial Press Ltd./Alamy*
Page 3, main: Dublin, August 2004. *Naki/Redferns/Getty Images.* **Inset:** Wristband from *21st Century Breakdown* tour, Houston, Texas, August 8, 2009.
Page 190: Duluth, Georgia, October 22, 2004. *Frank Mullen/WireImage/Getty Images*
Page 192: Back home in Oakland, April 14, 2009. *Araya Diaz/WireImage/Getty Images*
Background brushes: *Nathan Brown (www.room122.com)*

Acquisition and Project Editor: Dennis Pernu
Design Manager: Cindy Samargia Laun
Cover Designer: Simon Larkin
Interior Designer: Simon Larkin
Layout: Karl Laun

Printed in China